THE SMALL BUSINESS
FORM BOOK

KATHERINE L. DELSACK, ESQ.

LAWPREP PRESS, CALIFORNIA

LawPrep Press, a division of
LawPrep, Inc., a California corporation

© 1990 by

LawPrep Press
P.O. Box 7566
Newport Beach, California 92658

"This publication is designed to provide accurate
and authoritative information in regard to the subject matter
covered. It is sold with the understanding that the publisher
is not engaged in rendering legal, accounting, or other
professional services. If legal advice or other expert
assistance is required, the services of a competent
professional person should be sought."

*From the declaration of Principles jointly adopted by a Committee of the American Bar
Association and a Committee of Publishers and Associations.*

Printed in the United States of America

THE SMALL BUSINESS FORM BOOK

This book is designed to assist you in forming and running your corporate entity. It is aimed at the small, non-public, for-profit, stock corporation. While there are many formalities associated with the formation and maintenance of a corporation, this book will provide you with the necessary documents to comply with California law. This book is not intended to provide you with an explanation of the law. Rather, the book provides sample forms for use in conjunction with the advice you receive from your attorney.

CONTENTS

CHAPTER ONE

i

Minutes... 65

Resolutions... 77

CHAPTER TWO

CORPORATE MAINTENANCE.................................... 121

CHAPTER THREE

v

CHAPTER ONE

CORPORATE FORMATION

I. NAME RESERVATIONS

It is a good idea to check the availability of a desired name before filing the Articles of Incorporation. Merely filing the Articles of Incorporation does not guarantee that you will not be involved in a trade name infringement lawsuit. However, the filing of Articles of Incorporation does create a rebuttable presumption, meaning the Articles of Incorporation will be held as good evidence unless evidence to the contrary is introduced. So generally, the corporation is entitled to use the name if it filed the Articles of Incorporation using the name first, or obtained a tradename certificate from the State of California.

The Name Availability Unit, a section of the Secretary of State, checks proposed names for reservation. Upon written request for name reservation, the unit will check up to four names. The names should be listed in preferred order, with the request that the first available name be reserved. The fee is nominal. Reservations are made for 60 days and may be renewed by filing a new name reservation request with the Name Availability Unit.

Names can also be reserved "over the counter" at the main office in Sacramento or any of the satellite offices for a small fee.

A request for name availability can be done by a written request or by telephone. Up to four names will be checked upon written request and two names will be checked if you telephone the Secretary of State at **(916) 322-2387**.

II. FILING ARTICLES OF INCORPORATION

A corporation is formed when it files its Articles of Incorporation with the California Secretary of State.

Sections 200-202 of the California Corporations Code set forth the minimum requirements for filing the Articles of Incorporation. The Secretary of State does <u>not</u> require that a particular form be used for the incorporation of stock, for-profit corporations.

The Articles of Incorporation suggested in the California Corporations Code are the most basic Articles that will be accepted by the California Secretary of State for filing. There are a number of optional provisions which may be included, e.g., the number of directors, pre-emptive rights, cumulative voting, and indemnification provisions.

At a minimum the Articles of Incorporation must state:

1.   The name of the corporation.

The name must include not only the name but one of the following words: "corporation," "incorporated," "limited," or any abbreviation of one of those words.

2.   The purpose for which the corporation is formed.

Section 202 of the California Corporations Code provides a generic statement of purpose which is appropriate for most businesses.

3.   The name and address of an agent for service of process in the State of California.

4.   The number of shares of stock which are authorized to be issued by the corporation.

This may be any number of shares but the corporation may never issue more than the shares authorized in the Articles of Incorporation without an amendment to the Articles of Incorporation which requires a majority shareholder vote.

The following sample of Articles of Incorporation sets forth the essential information required by the Secretary of State. It is customary to accompany the Articles of Incorporation with a simple cover letter (see below) and a check covering the filing fees. Note that although your documents are filed upon receipt, you may not receive verification, for a few days or perhaps weeks. The enormous amount of filings received daily makes it virtually impossible for immediate verification unless you call the Secretary of State and find someone who can personally locate and identify your papers. There are a number of commercial corporate filing services who can hand-carry your documents to the Secretary of State's office, which often avoids such delays.

SAMPLE

ARTICLES OF INCORPORATION

ARTICLES OF INCORPORATION
OF
[NAME OF CORPORATION]

I.

The name of this corporation is _____

II.

The purpose of this corporation is to engage in any lawful act or activity for which a corporation may be organized under the General Corporation Law of California other than the banking business, the trust company business or the practice of a profession permitted to be incorporated by the California Corporations Code.

III.

The name and address in the State of California of this corporation's initial agent for service of process is:

_____

_____

_____.

IV.

This corporation is authorized to issue only one class of shares of stock; and the total number of shares which the corporation is authorized to issue is _____.

Dated: _____

_____,Incorporator

I hereby declare under penalty of perjury under the laws of the State of California that I am the person who executed the above Articles of Incorporation, and this instrument is my act and deed.

Dated: _____

_____,Incorporator

SAMPLE

<u>LETTER TO SECRETARY OF STATE</u>

Office of the Secretary of State of California
1230 J Street
Sacramento, California 95814

Re:_____,Inc.

To the Secretary of State:

    Please find enclosed Articles of Incorporation for _____ Inc.; three identical copies to be conformed and returned to my office; and a check in the sum of $ ____ to cover filing fees.

    If you have any difficulties or questions regarding this filing, please call me collect at _____.

    Thank you for your cooperation and assistance.

                Sincerely,

AMENDMENTS

Amendments to the Articles of Incorporation may be necessary for a number of reasons. They are particularly important if information in the original Articles of Incorporation must be changed. For example, if you originally state that there are 100,000 authorized shares of stock and you issue 50,000 to yourself and 50,000 to your brother than if your sister wants to own a certain number of shares there are no authorized shares remaining for the corporation to issue to her. Therefore, you must prepare an amendment to the Articles of Incorporation changing the authorized number of shares from 100,000 to a larger number.

The requirements for amending Articles of Incorporation are found in Sections 900-910 of the California Corporations Code. The amendment must satisfy the minimum requirements of Section 905 of the California Corporations Code, if the Certificate of Amendment is adopted after the issuance of shares. It is important to note that the format for the amendment to the Articles of Incorporation changes depending upon whether the amendment is adopted by the shareholders and directors or the directors alone.

The amendment must satisfy the minimum requirements of Section 906 of the California Corporations Code, if the Certificate of Amendment is adopted prior to the issuance of shares. In this event the Certificate of Amendment is executed by the incorporator.

The Certificate of Amendment must use the same roman numerals or numbering as is used in the original Articles of Incorporation. The Certificate of Amendment should also set forth the paragraph or section as it appears in the original Articles of Incorporation and then set forth the wording of the changed paragraph or section.

In instances in which the Certificate of Amendment is filed after the issuance of shares in the corporation, the President, Chairman of the Board or Vice-President and the Secretary, Assistant Secretary, Chief Financial Officer, Treasurer or Assistant Treasurer must sign the Certificate of Amendment.

Whether the Certificate of Amendment has been filed before of after the issuance of shares, it must be filed with the Secretary of State along with a fee. As a general rule, however, an amendment made after shares have been issued requires the approval of the outstanding shares (the present shareholders in the corporation).

SAMPLE

<u>CERTIFICATE OF AMENDMENT</u>

CERTIFICATE OF AMENDMENT
OF
ARTICLES OF INCORPORATION

_____ and _____ certify that:

1.   They are the president and the secretary, respectively, of
_____, a California Corporation.

2.   Article _____ of the articles of incorporation of this
corporation is amended to read as follows:

    [set forth the amended article]

3.   The foregoing amendment of articles of incorporation has been duly
approved by the board of directors.

4.   The foregoing amendment of articles of incorporation has been duly
approved by the required vote of shareholders in accordance with Section 902 of the
Corporations Code. The total number of outstanding shares of the corporation is
_____. The number of shares voting in favor of the amendment equaled or
exceeded the vote required. The percentage vote required was more than 50%.

Dated: _____

_____,President

_____,Secretary

       We further declare under penalty of perjury under the laws of the State of California that the matters set forth in this certificate are true and correct of our own knowledge.

Dated: _____

_____,President

_____,Secretary

THE SUBCHAPTER S ELECTION

Once the corporation is formed, it should be determined whether a subchapter S election can or should be made. The purpose of a subchapter S election is to permit taxpayers to select the corporate form of business without having the income of the business being taxed twice, once at the corporate level when earned and then again upon distribution to the shareholder.

Whether a corporation should elect this status is a question which should be discussed with both an attorney and an accountant. Once a subchapter S election is decided upon, the election must be made within 75 days after the corporation receives assets, begins doing business, or acquires shareholders, whichever occurs first.

The subchapter S election was initially enacted in 1958. It was designed to tax the taxable income of the corporation to the shareholders as dividends, whether distributed or retained by the corporation. Only capital gains were passed through to the shareholders. The system permitted subsequent distributions of previously taxed income without taxation to the shareholder. Although the election had tremendous advantages, extensive controls were imposed on eligibility to prevent tax abuse. Because of the intricate formulas and restrictions used to establish eligibility, many practitioners recommended its use only when absolutely necessary.

The Subchapter S Revision Act of 1982 was a comprehensive revision. The Act repealed the "dividend system" and extended many of the principles of partnership taxation to the subchapter S corporation and its shareholders. The Act simplified rules on eligibility, potential abuses were removed, and new entity audit procedures were established.

Subsequent acts have brought about more options. The Tax Reform Act of 1986 brought about two major changes. Both are related corporate taxation of appreciated property. The Revenue Act of 1987 permitted some S corporations to elect a taxable year other than a permitted year (i.e., a calendar year).

To understand how and when the Sub-chapter S election can be made, it is helpful to understand the basic tax difference between corporations and partnerships.

A sole proprietorship or partnership is not considered a separate entity, like a corporation. The individual owners or partners do not pay taxes on their net income. Rather, they pay tax on their pro rata share of the earnings from the business. A corporation is a separate entity and pays taxes in two ways. First, the corporation must report and pay taxes on its net income, whether or not all or any portion of that income is distributed to the owners. Second, if the income is distributed to the shareholders, each shareholder must pay income tax on his or her share.

The strict double tax burden would probably prevent many small corporations from doing business in corporate form. However, the Internal Revenue Service allows qualified small corporations to elect to be taxed as partnerships rather than as corporations and thus avoid double taxation. The IRS grants a subchapter S election based on the "behavior" of the business. If the behavior more nearly resembles that of a corporation than a partnership or trust, the IRS will deem the organization a corporation for federal tax purposes. The IRS uses 4 criteria for the characterization of a corporation: (i) continuity of life; (ii) centralization of management; (iii) limited liability; and (iv) free transferability of interest. Based on these criteria, a "corporation" for federal tax purposes can be an insurance company, a partnership, joint stock corporation, or trust.

The subchapter S election has three primary tax effects on shareholders. First, income is taxed to the shareholders as and when received. Second, any remaining corporate income is taxed to the shareholder at the end of a corporate year. Then the income is tax free if later distributed while the corporation still qualifies as a Subchapter S corporation to shareholders who pay the tax.

After making the election, the appropriate resolutions should be adopted by the board. In addition, each shareholder must sign and file a consent to the corporate election. It may also be appropriate to have an attorney consider the necessity and practicability of obtaining consent of spouses, particularly in a community property state such as California.

Briefly, to elect a Subchapter S status a corporation may not have more than 35 shareholders and the shareholders must be individuals. Usually the corporation must operate on a calendar year; in certain situations a fiscal year end may be elected by the corporation if approved by the Internal Revenue Service.

Below is a sample Subchapter S election form and a stockholders consent form. The sample Subchapter S election form requires generic corporation information. The stockholders consent form is a sample resolution to be included in the minutes of the first meeting.

SAMPLE

STOCKHOLDER'S CONSENT
TO
INITIAL SUBCHAPTER S ELECTION

We, the undersigned, being all the shareholders of _____ Inc., a California corporation with offices at _____ __ [address], hereby consent to the election by such corporation to be treated as a small business corporation under provisions of Subchapter S of the Internal Revenue Code of 1954, as amended.

The names and addresses of the undersigned, the number of shares owned by each, and the date or dates such shares were acquired, are as follows:

Name and Address	Number of Shares Owned	Date(s) Acquired
_____	_____	_____
_____	_____	_____
_____	_____	_____

Dated: ___, 19__

_____
Signature

_____
Signature

_____
Signature

BYLAWS

Once the Articles of Incorporation have been filed with the California Secretary of State and the appropriate filing fee and franchise tax deposit have been paid, the corporation is considered legally formed.

The next task is to prepare Bylaws for the corporation. Statutory requirements that a corporation adopt bylaws are implicit rather than explicit. Nevertheless, Bylaws are highly advisable to attain maximum flexibility and to establish optional voting controls and other provisions permitted by statute. California law requires only one bylaw provision, and that bylaw relates to the number of directors; the provision is only necessary, however, if the Articles of Incorporation do not contain the provision. Please note, that the minimum information required by the Secretary of State in the Articles of Incorporation does not require a provision for the number of directors.The rule is that the number of directors must equal the number of shareholders up to three; beyond that, only three directors are needed, no matter how many shareholders there are.

Bylaws contain the corporation's operating rules and procedures. The Bylaws contain a variety of provisions, including those required by Section 212 of the California Corporations Code. The Bylaws also define the voting rights of shareholders and the procedure for holding meetings as well as notice requirements.

The requirements for shareholders' meetings, consents and voting rights are set forth in Sections 600-605 and 700-709 of the California Corporations Code. The Bylaws must also contain a description of the rights and duties of directors and management.

These minimum requirements are set forth in Sections 300-317 of the California Corporations Code. It is important to note that the California Corporations Code usually sets forth minimum requirements and these requirements can be modified, extended or narrowed depending upon the circumstances.

Please note, that the only information which needs to be completed in the Bylaws is in Article III, Section 2 pertaining to the number of directors.

SAMPLE

<u>BYLAWS</u>

BYLAWS

OF

_____

ARTICLE I.

OFFICES

Section 1. PRINCIPAL OFFICES. The Board of Directors shall fix the location of the principal executive office of the Corporation at any place within or outside the State of California. If the principal executive office is located outside this state, and the Corporation has one or more business offices in this state, the Board of Directors shall likewise fix and designate a principal business office in the State of California.

Section 2. OTHER OFFICES. The Board of Directors may at any time establish branch or subordinate offices at any place or places where the Corporation is qualified to do business.

ARTICLE II.

MEETINGS OF SHAREHOLDERS

Section 1. PLACE OF MEETINGS. Meetings of shareholders shall be held at any place within or outside the State of California designated by the Board of Directors. In the absence of any such designation, shareholders' meetings shall be held at the principal executive office of the Corporation.

Section 2. ANNUAL MEETINGS OF SHAREHOLDERS. The annual meeting of shareholders shall be held each year on a date and at a time designated by the Board of Directors. At each annual meeting, directors shall be elected and any other proper business may be transacted.

Section 3. SPECIAL MEETINGS. A special meeting of shareholders may be called at any time by the Board of Directors, or by the chairman of the board, or by the president, or by one or more shareholders holding shares in the aggregate entitled to cast not less than 10% of the votes at any such meeting.

If a special meeting is called by any person or persons other than the Board of Directors, the request shall be in writing, specifying the time of such meeting and the general nature of the business proposed to be transacted, and shall be delivered personally or sent by registered mail or by telegraphic or other facsimile transmission to the chairman of the board, the president, any vice president or the secretary of the Corporation. The officer receiving such request forthwith shall cause notice to be given to the shareholders entitled to vote, in accordance with the provisions of this Article II, that a meeting will be held at the time requested by the person or persons calling the meeting, not less than thirty-five (35) nor more than sixty (60) days after the receipt of the request. If the notice is not given within twenty (20) days after receipt of the request, the person or persons requesting the meeting may give the notice. Nothing contained in this paragraph of this Section 3 shall be construed as limiting, fixing or affecting the time when a meeting of shareholders called by action of the Board of Directors may be held.

Section 4. NOTICE OF SHAREHOLDERS' MEETINGS. All notices of meetings of shareholders shall be sent or otherwise given in accordance with Section 5 of this Article II not less than ten (10) nor more than sixty (60) days before the date of the meeting being noticed. The notice shall specify the place, date and hour of the meeting and (i) in the case of a special meeting, the general nature of the business to be transacted, or (ii) in the case of the annual meeting, those matters which the Board of Directors, at the time of giving the notice, intends to present for action by the shareholders. The notice of any meeting at which directors are to be elected shall include the name of any nominee or nominees which, at the time of the notice, the Board of Directors intends to present for election.

If action is proposed to be taken at any meeting for approval of (i) a contract or transaction in which a director has a direct or indirect financial interest, pursuant to Section 310 of the Corporations Code of California, (ii) an amendment of the articles of incorporation, pursuant to Section 902 of such Code, (iii) a reorganization of the Corporation, pursuant to Section 1201 of such Code, (iv) a voluntary dissolution of the Corporation, pursuant to Section 1900 of such Code, or

(v) a distribution in dissolution other than in accordance with the rights of outstanding preferred shares, pursuant to Section 2007 of such Code, the notice shall also state the general nature of such proposal.

Section 5. MANNER OF GIVING NOTICE; AFFIDAVIT OF NOTICE. Notice of any meeting of shareholders shall be given either personally or by first-class mail or telegraphic or other written communication, charges prepaid, addressed to the shareholder at the address of such shareholder appearing on the books of the Corporation or given by the shareholder to the Corporation for the purpose of notice. If no such address appears on the Corporation's books or is given, notice shall be deemed to have been given if sent by mail or telegram to the Corporation's principal executive office, or if published at least once in a newspaper of general circulation in the county where this office is located. Notice shall be deemed to have been given at the time when delivered personally or deposited in the mail or sent by telegram or other means of written communication.

If any notice addressed to a shareholder at the address of such shareholder appearing on the books of the Corporation is returned to the Corporation by the United States Postal Service marked to indicate that the United States Postal Service is unable to deliver the notice to the shareholder at such address, all future notices or reports shall be deemed to have been duly given without further mailing if the same shall be available to the shareholder upon written demand of the shareholder at the principal executive office of the Corporation for a period of one year from the date of the giving of such notice.

An affidavit of the mailing or other means of giving any notice of any shareholders' meeting shall be executed by the secretary, assistant secretary or any transfer agent of the Corporation giving such notice, and shall be filed and maintained in the minute book of the Corporation.

Section 6. QUORUM. The presence in person or by proxy of the holders of a majority of the shares entitled to vote at a meeting of shareholders shall constitute a quorum for the transaction of business. The shareholders present at a duly called or held meeting at which a quorum is present may continue to do business until adjournment, notwithstanding the withdrawal of enough shareholders to leave less than a quorum, if any action taken (other than adjournment) is approved by at least a majority of the shares required to constitute a quorum.

Section 7. ADJOURNED MEETING AND NOTICE THEREOF. Any shareholders' meeting, annual or special, whether or not a quorum is present, may be adjourned from time to time by the vote of the majority of the shares represented at such meeting, either in person or by proxy, but in the absence of a quorum, no other business may be transacted at such meeting, except as provided in this Article II.

When any meeting of shareholders, either annual or special, is adjourned to another time or place, notice need not be given of the adjourned meeting if the time and place thereof are announced at a meeting at which the adjournment is taken, unless a new record date for the adjourned meeting is fixed, or unless the adjournment is for more than forty five (45) days from the date set for the original meeting, in which case the Board of Directors shall set a new record date. Notice of any such adjourned meeting shall be given to each shareholder of record entitled to vote at the adjourned meeting in accordance with the provisions of this Article II. At any adjourned meeting the Corporation may transact any business which might have been transacted at the original meeting.

Section 8. VOTING. The shareholders entitled to vote at any meeting of shareholders shall be determined in accordance with the provisions of Section 11 of this Article II, subject to the provisions of Sections 702 to 704, inclusive, of the Corporations Code of California (relating to voting shares held by a fiduciary, in the name of a corporation or in joint ownership). Such vote may be by voice vote or by ballot; provided, however, that all elections for directors must be by ballot upon demand by a shareholder at any election and before the voting begins. Any shareholder entitled to vote on any matter (other than elections of directors) may vote part of the shares in favor of the proposal and refrain from voting the remaining shares or vote them against the proposal, but, if the shareholder fails to specify the number of shares such shareholder is voting affirmatively, it will be conclusively presumed that the shareholder's approving vote is with respect to all shares such shareholder is entitled to vote. Except as provided in this Article II, the affirmative vote of a majority of the shares represented and voting at a duly held meeting at which a quorum is present (which shares voting affirmatively also constitute at least a majority of the required quorum) shall be the act of the shareholders, unless the vote of a greater number or voting by classes is required by the California General Corporation Law or the Articles of Incorporation.

At a shareholders' meeting involving the election of directors, no shareholder shall be entitled to cumulate votes (i.e., cast for any candidate a number of votes greater than the number of votes which such shareholder normally is entitled to cast) unless such candidate or candidates' names have been placed in nomination prior to the voting and a shareholder has given notice at the meeting prior to the voting of the shareholder's intention to cumulate votes. If any shareholder has given such notice, then every shareholder entitled to vote may cumulate such shareholder's votes for candidates in nomination and give one candidate a number of votes equal to the number of directors to be elected multiplied by the number of votes to which such shareholder's shares are normally entitled, or distribute the shareholder's votes on the same principle among any or all of the candidates, as the shareholder thinks fit. The candidates receiving the highest number of affirmative votes up to the number of directors to be elected, shall be elected. Votes against a director and votes withheld shall have no legal effect.

Section 9. WAIVER OF NOTICE OR CONSENT BY ABSENT SHAREHOLDERS. The transactions at any meeting of shareholders, either annual or special, however called and noticed, and wherever held, shall be as valid as though had at a meeting duly held after regular call and notice, if a quorum be present either in person or by proxy, and if, either before or after the meeting, each person entitled to vote, not present in person or by proxy, signs a written waiver of notice or a consent to a holding of the meeting, or an approval of the minutes thereof. The waiver of notice, consent to the holding of the meeting or approval of the minutes thereof need not specify either the business to be transacted or the purpose of any annual or special meeting of shareholders, except that if action is taken or proposed to be taken for approval of any of those matters specified in the second paragraph of Section 4 of this Article II, the waiver of notice, consent to the holding of the meeting or approval of the minutes thereof shall state the general nature of such proposal. All such waivers, consents or approvals shall be filed with the corporate records or made a part of the minutes of the meeting.

Attendance of a person at a meeting shall also constitute a waiver of notice of and presence at such meeting, except when the person objects, at the beginning of the meeting, to the transaction of any business because the meeting is not lawfully called or convened, and except that attendance at a meeting is not a waiver of any right to object to the consideration of matters required by the General Corporation Law to be included in the notice but which were not included in the notice, if such objection is expressly made at the meeting.

Section 10. SHAREHOLDER ACTION BY WRITTEN CONSENT WITHOUT A MEETING. Any action which may be taken at any annual or special meeting of shareholders may be taken without a meeting and without prior notice, if a consent in writing, setting forth the action so taken, is signed by the holders of outstanding shares having not less than the minimum number of votes that would be necessary to authorize or take such action at a meeting at which all shares entitled to vote thereon were present and voted. In the case of election of directors, such consent shall be effective only if signed by the holders of all outstanding shares entitled to vote for the election of directors; provided, however, that a director may be elected at any time to fill a vacancy not filled by the directors by the written consent of the holders of a majority of the outstanding shares entitled to vote for the election of directors. All such consents shall be filed with the secretary of the Corporation and shall be maintained in the corporate records. Any shareholder giving a written consent, or the shareholder's proxy holders, or a transferee of the shares or a personal representative of the shareholder or their respective proxy holders, may revoke the consent by a writing received by the secretary of the Corporation prior to the time that written consents of the number of shares required to authorize the proposed action have been filed with the secretary.

If the consents of all shareholders entitled to vote have not been solicited in writing, and if the unanimous written consent of all such shareholders shall not have been received, the secretary shall give prompt notice of the corporate action approved by the shareholders without a meeting. Such notice shall be given in the manner specified in Section 5 of this Article II. In the case of approval of (i) contracts or transactions in which a director has a direct or indirect financial interest, pursuant to Section 310 of the Corporations Code of California, (ii) indemnification of agents of the Corporation, pursuant to Section 317 of such Code, (iii) a reorganization of the Corporation, pursuant to Section 1201 of such Code, and (iv) a distribution in dissolution other than in accordance with the rights of outstanding preferred shares, pursuant to Section 2007 of such Code, such notice shall be given at least ten (10) days before the consummation of any such action authorized by any such approval.

Section 11. RECORD DATE FOR SHAREHOLDER NOTICE, VOTING, AND GIVING CONSENTS. For purposes of determining the shareholders entitled to notice of any meeting or to vote or entitled to give consent to corporate action without a meeting, the Board of Directors may fix, in advance, a record date, which shall not be more than sixty (60) days nor less than ten (10) days prior to the date of any such meeting nor more than sixty (60) days prior to such action without a meeting, and in such case only shareholders at the close of business on the record date so fixed are entitled to notice and to vote or to give consents, as the case may be, notwithstanding any transfer of any shares on the books of the Corporation after the record date fixed as aforesaid, except as otherwise provided in the California General Corporation Law.

If the Board of Directors does not so fix a record date:

1.   The record date for determining shareholders entitled to notice of or to vote at a meeting of shareholders shall be at the close of business on the business day next preceding the day on which notice is given or, if notice is waived, at the close of business on the business day next preceding the day on which the meeting is held.

2.   The record date for determining shareholders entitled to give consent to corporate action in writing without a meeting, (i) when no prior action by the board has been taken, shall be the day on which the first written consent is given, or (ii) when prior action of the board has been taken, shall be at the close of business on the day on which the board adopts the resolution relating thereto, or the sixtieth (60th) day prior to the date of such other action, whichever is later.

Section 12. PROXIES. Every person entitled to vote for directors or on any other matter shall have the right to do so either in person or by one or more agents authorized by a written proxy signed by the person and filed with the secretary of the Corporation. A proxy shall be deemed signed if the shareholder's name is placed on the proxy (whether by manual signature, typewriting, telegraphic transmission or otherwise) by the shareholder or the shareholder's attorney in fact. A validly executed proxy which does not state that it is irrevocable shall continue in full force and effect unless (i) revoked by the person executing it, prior to the vote pursuant thereto, by a writing delivered to the Corporation stating that the proxy is revoked or by a subsequent proxy executed by the person executing the prior proxy and presented to the meeting, or as to any meeting by attendance at such meeting and voting in person by the person executing the proxy; or (ii) written notice of the death or incapacity of the maker of such proxy is received by the Corporation before the vote pursuant thereto is counted; provided, however, that no such proxy shall be valid after the expiration of eleven (11) months from the date of such proxy, unless otherwise provided in the proxy. The revocability of a proxy that states on its face that it is irrevocable shall be governed by the provisions of Section 705(e) and (f) of the Corporations Code of California.

Section 13. INSPECTORS OF ELECTION. Before any meeting of shareholders, the Board of Directors may appoint any persons other than nominees for office to act as inspectors of election at the meeting or its adjournment. If no inspectors of election are so appointed, the chairman of the meeting may, and on the request of any shareholder or a shareholder's proxy shall, appoint inspectors of election at the meeting. The number of inspectors shall be either one (1) or three (3). If inspectors are appointed at a meeting on the request of one or more shareholders or proxies, the holders of a majority of shares or their proxies present at the meeting shall determine whether one (1) or three (3) inspectors are to be appointed. If any person appointed as inspector fails to appear or fails or refuses to act, the chairman of the meeting may, and upon the request of any shareholder or a shareholder's proxy shall, appoint a person to fill such vacancy.

The duties of these inspectors shall be as follows:

1. Determine the number of shares outstanding and the voting power of each, the shares represented at the meeting, the existence of a quorum, and the authenticity, validity and effect of proxies;

2. Receive votes, ballots or consents;

3. Hear and determine all challenges and questions in any way arising in connection with the right to vote;

4. Count and tabulate all votes or consents;

5. Determine when the polls shall close;

6. Determine the result; and

7. Do any other acts that may be proper to conduct the election or vote with fairness to all shareholders.

ARTICLE III.

DIRECTORS

Section 1. POWERS. Subject to the provisions of the California General Corporation Law and any limitations in the articles of incorporation and these bylaws relating to action required to be approved by the shareholders or by the outstanding shares, the business and affairs of the Corporation shall be managed and all corporate powers shall be exercised by or under the direction of the Board of Directors.

Without prejudice to such general powers, but subject to the same limitations, it is hereby expressly declared that the directors shall have the power and authority to:

1. Select and remove all officers, agents, and employees of the Corporation, prescribe such powers and duties for them as may not be inconsistent with law, with the articles of incorporation or these bylaws, fix their compensation, and require from them security for faithful service.

2.   Change the principal executive office or the principal business office in the State of California from one location to another; cause the Corporation to be qualified to do business in any other state, territory, dependency, or foreign country and conduct business within or outside the State of California; designate any place within or without the State of California for the holding of any shareholders' meeting, or meetings, including annual meetings; adopt, make and use a corporate seal, and prescribe the forms of certificates of stock, and alter the form of such seal and of such certificates from time to time as in their judgment they may deem best, provided that such forms shall at all times comply with the provisions of law.

3.   Authorize the issuance of shares of stock of the Corporation from time to time, upon such terms as may be lawful, in consideration of money paid, labor done or services actually rendered, debts or securities cancelled or tangible or intangible property actually received.

4.   Borrow money and incur indebtedness for the purposes of the Corporation, and cause to be executed and delivered therefor, in the corporate name, promissory notes, bonds, debentures, deeds of trust, mortgages, pledges, hypothecation, or other evidences of debt and securities therefor.

Section 2. NUMBER AND QUALIFICATION OF DIRECTORS. The authorized number of directors shall be ____ until changed by a duly adopted amendment to the articles of incorporation or by an amendment to this bylaw adopted by the vote or written consent of holders of a majority of the outstanding shares entitled to vote.

Section 3.   ELECTION AND TERM OF OFFICE OF DIRECTORS. Directors shall be elected at each annual meeting of the shareholders to hold office until the next annual meeting. Each director, including a director elected to fill a vacancy, shall hold office until the expiration of the term for which elected and until a successor has been elected and qualified.

Section 4. VACANCIES. Vacancies on the Board of Directors may be filled by a majority of the remaining directors, though less than a quorum, or by a sole remaining director, except that a vacancy created by the removal of a director by the vote or written consent of the shareholders or by court order may be filled only by the vote of a majority of the shares represented and voting at a duly held meeting at which a quorum is present (which shares voting affirmatively also constitute at least a majority of the required quorum) or by the written consent of holders of a majority of the outstanding shares entitled to vote. Each director so elected shall hold office until the next annual meeting of the shareholders and until a successor has been elected and qualified.

A vacancy or vacancies in the Board of Directors shall be deemed to exist in the case of the death, resignation or removal of any director, or if the Board of Directors by resolution declares vacant the office of a director who has been declared of unsound mind by an order of court or convicted of a felony, or if the authorized number of directors be increased, or if the shareholders fail at any meeting of shareholders at which any director or directors are elected, to elect the full authorized number of directors to be voted for at that meeting.

The shareholders may elect a director or directors at any time to fill any vacancy or vacancies not filled by the directors, but any such election by written consent shall require the consent of a majority of the outstanding shares entitled to vote.

Any director may resign effective upon giving written notice to the chairman of the board, the president, the secretary or the Board of Directors, unless the notice specifies a later time for the effectiveness of such resignation. If the resignation of a director is effective at a future time, the Board of Directors may elect a successor to take office when the resignation becomes effective.

No reduction of the authorized number of directors shall have the effect of removing any director prior to the expiration of his term of office.

Section 5.   PLACE OF MEETINGS AND TELEPHONIC MEETINGS. Regular meetings of the Board of Directors may be held at any place within or without the State of California that has been designated from time to time by resolution of the board. In the absence of such designation, regular meetings shall be held at the principal executive office of the Corporation. Special meetings of the board shall be held at any place within or without the State of California that has been designated in the notice of the meeting or, if not stated in the notice or there is no notice, at the principal executive office of the Corporation. Any meeting, regular or special, may be held by conference telephone or similar communication equipment, so long as all directors participating in such meeting can hear one another, and all such directors shall be deemed to be present in person at such meeting.

Section 6. ANNUAL MEETING. Immediately following each annual meeting of shareholders, the Board of Directors shall hold a regular meeting for the purpose of organization, any desired election of officers and the transaction of other business. Notice of this meeting shall not be required.

Section 7. OTHER REGULAR MEETINGS. Other regular meetings of the Board of Directors shall be held without call at such time as shall from time to time be fixed by the Board of Directors. Such regular meetings may be held without notice.

Section 8. SPECIAL MEETINGS. Special meetings of the Board of Directors for any purpose or purposes may be called at any time by the chairman of the board or the president or any vice president or the secretary or any two directors.

Notice of the time and place of special meetings shall be delivered personally or by telephone to each director or sent by first-class mail or telegram, charges pre-paid, addressed to each director at his or her address as it is shown upon the records of the Corporation. In case such notice is mailed, it shall be deposited in the United States mail at least four (4) days prior to the time of the holding of the meeting. In case such notice is delivered personally, or by telephone or telegram, it shall be delivered personally or by telephone or to the telegraph company at least forty-eight (48) hours prior to the time of the holding of the meeting. Any oral notice given personally or by telephone may be communicated to either the director or to a person at the office of the director who the person giving the notice has reason to believe will promptly communicate it to the director. The notice need not specify the purpose of the meeting nor the place if the meeting is to be held at the principal executive office of the Corporation.

Section 9. QUORUM. A majority of the authorized number of directors shall constitute a quorum for the transaction of business, except to adjourn as hereinafter provided. Every act or decision done or made by a majority of the directors present at a meeting duly held at which a quorum is present shall be regarded as the act of the Board of Directors, subject to the provisions of Section 310 of the Corporations Code of California (approval of contracts or transactions in which a director has a direct or indirect material financial interest), Section 311 of that Code (appointment of committees), and Section 317(e) of that Code (indemnification of directors). A meeting at which a quorum is initially present may continue to transact business notwithstanding the withdrawal of directors, if any action taken is approved by at least a majority of the required quorum for such meeting.

Section 10. WAIVER OF NOTICE. Notice of a meeting need not be given to any director who signs a waiver of notice or a consent to holding the meeting or an approval of the minutes thereof, whether before or after the meeting, or who attends the meeting without protesting, prior thereto or at its commencement, the lack of notice. The waiver of notice or consent need not specify the purpose of the meeting. All such waivers, consents and approvals shall be filed with the corporate records or made a part of the minutes of the meeting.

Section 11. ADJOURNMENT. A majority of the directors present, whether or not constituting a quorum, may adjourn any meeting to another time and place.

Section 12. NOTICE OF ADJOURNMENT. Notice of the time and place of holding an adjourned meeting need not be given, unless the meeting is adjourned for more than twenty-four hours, in which case notice of such time and place shall be given prior to the time of the adjourned meeting, in the manner specified in Section 8 of this Article III, to the directors who were not present at the time of the adjournment.

Section 13. ACTION WITHOUT MEETING. Any action required or permitted to be taken by the Board of Directors may be taken without a meeting, if all members of the board shall individually or collectively consent in writing to such action. Such action by written consent shall have the same force and effect as a unanimous vote of the Board of Directors. Such written consent or consents shall be filed with the minutes of the proceedings of the board.

Section 14. FEES AND COMPENSATION OF DIRECTORS. Directors and members of committees may receive such compensation, if any, for their services, and such reimbursement of expenses, as may be fixed or determined by resolution of the Board of Directors. Nothing contained herein shall be construed to preclude any director from serving the Corporation in any other capacity as an officer, agent, employee, or otherwise, and receiving compensation for such services.

ARTICLE IV.

COMMITTEES

Section 1. COMMITTEES OF DIRECTORS. The Board of Directors may, by resolution adopted by a majority of the authorized number of directors, designate one or more committees, each consisting of two or more directors, to serve at the pleasure of the board. The board may designate one or more directors as alternate members of any committee, who may replace any absent member at any meeting of the committee. The appointment of members or alternate members of a committee requires the vote of a majority of the authorized number of directors. Any such committee, to the extent provided in the resolution of the board, shall have all the authority of the board, except with respect to:

1. The approval of any action which, under the General Corporation Law of California, also requires shareholders' approval or approval of the outstanding shares;

2. The filling of vacancies on the Board of Directors or in any committee;

3. The fixing of compensation of the directors for serving on the board or on any committee;

4. The amendment or repeal of bylaws or the adoption of new bylaws;

5. The amendment or repeal of any resolution of the Board of Directors which by its express terms is not so amendable or repealable;

6. A distribution to the shareholders of the Corporation, except at a rate or in a periodic amount or within a price range determined by the Board of Directors; or

7. The appointment of any other committees of the Board of Directors or the members thereof.

Section 2. MEETINGS AND ACTION OF COMMITTEES. Meetings and action of committees shall be governed by, and held and taken in accordance with, the provisions of Article III of these bylaws, Sections 5 (place of meetings), 7 (regular meetings), 8 (special meetings and notice), 9 (quorum), 10 (waiver of notice), 11 (adjournment), 12 (notice of adjournment) and 13 (action without meeting), with such changes in the context of those bylaws as are necessary to substitute the committee and its members for the Board of Directors and its members, except that the time of regular meetings of committees may be determined by resolution of the Board of Directors as well as by resolution of the committee; special meetings of committees may also be called by resolution of the Board of Directors; and notice of special meetings of committees shall also be given to all alternate members, who shall have the right to attend all meetings of the committee. The Board of Directors may adopt rules for the government of any committee not inconsistent with the provisions of these bylaws.

ARTICLE V.

OFFICERS

Section 1. OFFICERS. The officers of the Corporation shall be a president, an executive vice president, a secretary and a chief financial officer. The Corporation may also have, at the discretion of the Board of Directors, a chairman of the board, one or more additional vice-presidents, one or more assistant secretaries, one or more assistant chief financial officers, and such other officers as may be appointed in accordance with the provisions of Section 3 of this Article V. Any number of offices may be held by the same person.

Section 2. ELECTION OF OFFICERS. The officers of the Corporation, except such officers as may be appointed in accordance with the provisions of Section 3 or Section 5 of this Article V, shall be chosen by the Board of Directors, and each shall serve at the pleasure of the board, subject to the rights, if any, of an officer under any contract of employment.

Section 3. SUBORDINATE OFFICERS, ETC. The Board of Directors may appoint, and may empower the president to appoint, such other officers as the business of the Corporation may require, each of whom shall hold office for such period, have such authority and perform such duties as are provided in the Bylaws or as the Board of Directors may from time to time determine.

Section 4. REMOVAL AND RESIGNATION OF OFFICERS. Subject to the rights, if any, of an officer under any contract of employment, any officer may be removed, either with or without cause, by the Board of Directors, at any regular or special meeting thereof, or, except in case of an officer chosen by the Board of Directors, by any officer upon whom such power of removal may be conferred by the Board of Directors.

Any officer may resign at any time by giving written notice to the Corporation. Any such resignation shall take effect at the date of the receipt of such notice or at any later time specified therein; and, unless otherwise specified therein, the acceptance of such resignation shall not be necessary to make it effective. Any such resignation is without prejudice to the rights, if any, of the Corporation under any contract to which the officer is a party.

Section 5. VACANCIES IN OFFICES. A vacancy in any office because of death, resignation, removal, disqualification or any other cause shall be filled in the manner prescribed in these bylaws for regular appointments to such office.

Section 6. CHAIRMAN OF THE BOARD. The chairman of the board, if such an officer be elected, shall, if present, preside at all meetings of the Board of Directors and exercise and perform such other powers and duties as may be from time to time assigned to him by the Board of Directors or prescribed by the bylaws. If there is no president, the chairman of the board shall in addition be the chief executive officer of the Corporation and shall have the powers and duties prescribed in Section 7 of this Article V.

Section 7. PRESIDENT. Subject to such supervisory powers, if any, as may be given by the Board of Directors to the chairman of the board, if there be such an officer, the president shall be the chief executive officer of the Corporation and shall, subject to the control of the Board of Directors, have general supervision, direction and control of the business and the officers of the Corporation. He shall preside at all meetings of the shareholders and, in the absence of the chairman of the board, or if there be none, at all meetings of the Board of Directors. He shall have the general powers and duties of management usually vested in the office of president of a Corporation, and shall have such other powers and duties as may be prescribed by the Board of Directors or the Bylaws.

Section 8. VICE PRESIDENTS. In the absence or disability of the president, the vice presidents, if any, in order of their rank as fixed by the Board of Directors or, if not ranked, a vice president designated by the Board of Directors, shall perform all the duties of the president, and when so acting shall have all the powers of, and be subject to all restrictions upon, the president. The vice president shall have such other powers and perform such other duties as from time to time may be prescribed for them respectively by the Board of Directors or the Bylaws, the president or the chairman of the board.

Section 9. SECRETARY. The secretary shall keep or cause to be kept, at the principal executive office or such other place as the Board of Directors may order, a book of minutes of all meetings and actions of directors, committees of directors and shareholders, with the time and place of holding, whether regular or special, and, if special, how authorized, the notice thereof given, the names of those present at directors' and committee meetings, the number of shares present or represented at shareholders' meetings, and the proceedings thereof.

The secretary shall keep, or cause to be kept, at the principal executive office or at the office of the Corporation's transfer agent or registrar, as determined by resolution of the Board of Directors, a share register, or a duplicate share register, showing the names of all shareholders and their addresses, the number and classes of shares held by each, the number and date of certificates issued for the same, and the number and date of cancellation of every certificate surrendered for cancellation.

The secretary shall give, or cause to be given, notice of all meetings of the shareholders and of the Board of Directors required by the Bylaws or by law to be given, and he shall keep the seal of the Corporation, if one be adopted, in safe custody, and shall have such other powers and perform such other duties as may be prescribed by the Board of Directors or by the Bylaws.

Section 10. CHIEF FINANCIAL OFFICER. The chief financial officer shall keep and maintain, or cause to be kept and maintained, adequate and correct books and records of accounts of the properties and business transactions of the Corporation, including accounts of its assets, liabilities, receipts, disbursements, gains, losses, capital, retained earnings and shares. The books of account shall at all reasonable times be open to inspection by any director.

The chief financial officer shall deposit all moneys and other valuables in the name and to the credit of the Corporation with such depositaries as may be designated by the Board of Directors. He shall disburse the funds of the Corporation as may be ordered by the Board of Directors, shall render to the president and directors, whenever they request it, an account of all of his transactions as chief financial officer and of the financial condition of the Corporation, and shall have such other powers and perform such other duties as may be prescribed by the Board of Directors or the Bylaws.

Section 11. REIMBURSEMENT OF CORPORATION. Any payments made to an officer of the Corporation such as a salary, commission, bonus, interest, or rent, or entertainment expense incurred by him, which shall be disallowed in whole or in part as a deductible expense by the Internal Revenue Service, shall be reimbursed by such officer to the Corporation to the full extent of such disallowance. It shall be the duty of the board to enforce payment of each such amount disallowed. In lieu of payment by the officer, subject to the determination of the board, proportionate amounts may be withheld from his future compensation payments until the amount owed to the Corporation has been recovered.

ARTICLE VI.

INDEMNIFICATION OF DIRECTORS, OFFICERS, EMPLOYEES AND OTHER AGENTS

Section 1.   INDEMNIFICATION - THIRD PARTY PROCEEDINGS. The Corporation shall indemnify any person (the "Indemnitee") who is or was a party or is threatened to be made a party to any proceeding (other than an action by or in the right of the Corporation to procure a judgment in its favor) by reason of the fact that Indemnitee is or was a director or officer of the Corporation, or any subsidiary of the Corporation, and the Corporation may indemnify a person who is or was a party or is threatened to be made a party to any proceeding (other than an action by or in the right of the Corporation to procure a judgment in its favor) by reason of the fact that such person is or was an employee or other agent of the Corporation (the "Indemnitee Agent") by reason of any action or inaction on the part of Indemnitee or Indemnitee Agent while an officer, director or agent or by reason of the fact that Indemnitee or Indemnitee Agent is or was serving at the request of the Corporation as a director, officer, employee or agent of another Corporation, partnership, joint venture, trust or other enterprise, against expenses (including subject to Section 19, attorneys' fees and any expenses of establishing a right to indemnification pursuant to this Article VI or under California law), judgments, fines, settlements (if such settlement is approved in advance by the Corporation, which approval shall not be unreasonably withheld) and other amounts actually and reasonably incurred by Indemnitee or Indemnitee Agent in connection with such proceeding if Indemnitee or Indemnitee Agent acted in good faith and in a manner Indemnitee or Indemnitee Agent reasonably believed to be in or not opposed to the best interests of the Corporation and, in the case of a criminal proceeding, if Indemnitee or Indemnitee Agent had no reasonable cause to believe Indemnitee's or Indemnitee Agent's conduct was unlawful.

The termination of any proceeding by judgment, order, settlement, conviction or upon a plea of nolo contendere or its equivalent shall not, of itself, create a presumption that Indemnitee or Indemnitee Agent did not act in good faith and in a manner which Indemnitee or Indemnitee Agent reasonably believed to be in or not opposed to the best interests of the Corporation, or with respect to any criminal proceedings, would not create a presumption that Indemnitee or Indemnitee Agent had reasonable cause to believe that Indemnitee's or Indemnitee Agent's conduct was unlawful.

Section 2. INDEMNIFICATION - PROCEEDINGS BY OR IN THE RIGHT OF THE CORPORATION. The Corporation shall indemnify Indemnitee and may indemnify Indemnitee Agent if Indemnitee, or Indemnitee Agent, as the case may be, was or is a party or is threatened to be made a party to any threatened, pending or completed action by or in the right of the Corporation or any subsidiary of the Corporation to procure a judgment in its favor by reason of the fact that Indemnitee or Indemnitee Agent is or was a director, officer, employee or other agent of the Corporation, or any subsidiary of the Corporation, by reason of any action or inaction on the part of Indemnitee or Indemnitee Agent while an officer, director or agent or by reason of the fact that Indemnitee or Indemnitee Agent is or was serving at the request of the Corporation as a director, officer, employee or agent of another Corporation, partnership, joint venture, trust or other enterprise, against expenses (including subject to Section 19, attorneys' fees and any expenses of establishing a right to indemnification pursuant to this Article VI or under California law) and, to the fullest extent permitted by law, amounts paid in settlement, in each case to the extent actually and reasonably incurred by Indemnitee or Indemnitee Agent in connection with the defense or settlement of the proceeding if Indemnitee or Indemnitee Agent acted in good faith and in a manner Indemnitee or Indemnitee Agent believed to be in or not opposed to the best interests of the Corporation and its shareholders, except that no indemnification shall be made with respect to any claim, issue or matter to which Indemnitee (or Indemnitee Agent) shall have been adjudged to have been liable to the Corporation in the performance of Indemnitee's or Indemnitee Agent's duty to the Corporation and its shareholders, unless and only to the extent that the court in which such proceeding is or was pending shall determine upon application that, in view of all the circumstances of the case, Indemnitee (or Indemnitee Agent) is fairly and reasonably entitled to indemnity for expenses and then only to the extent that the court shall determine.

Section 3. SUCCESSFUL DEFENSE ON MERITS. To the extent that Indemnitee (or Indemnitee Agent) without limitation has been successful on the merits in defense of any proceeding referred to in Sections 1 or 2 above, or in defense of any claim, issue or matter therein, the Corporation shall indemnify Indemnitee (or Indemnitee Agent) against expenses (including attorneys' fees) actually and reasonably incurred by Indemnitee (or Indemnitee Agent) in connection therewith.

Section 4. CERTAIN TERMS DEFINED. For purposes of this Article VI, references to "other enterprises" shall include employee benefit plans, references to "fines" shall include any excise taxes assessed on Indemnitee or Indemnitee Agent with respect to an employee benefit plan, and references to "proceeding" shall include any threatened, pending or completed action or proceeding, whether civil, criminal, administrative or investigative. References to "Corporation" include all constituent Corporations absorbed in a consolidation or merger as well as the resulting or surviving Corporation, so that any person who is or was a director, officer, employee, or other agent of such a constituent Corporation or who, being or having been such a director, officer, employee or other agent of another Corporation, partnership, joint venture, trust or other enterprise shall stand in the same position under the provisions of this Article VI with respect to the resulting or surviving Corporation as such person would if he or she had served the resulting or surviving Corporation in the same capacity.

Section 5. ADVANCEMENT OF EXPENSES. The Corporation shall advance all expenses incurred by Indemnitee and may advance all or any expenses incurred by Indemnitee Agent in connection with the investigation, defense, settlement (excluding amounts actually paid in settlement of any action, suit or proceeding) or appeal of any civil or criminal action, suit or proceeding referenced in Sections 1 or 2 hereof. Indemnitee or Indemnitee Agent hereby undertakes to repay such amounts advanced only if, and to the extent that, it shall be determined ultimately that Indemnitee or Indemnitee Agent is not entitled to be indemnified by the Corporation as authorized hereby. The advances to be made hereunder shall be paid by the Corporation (i) to Indemnitee within twenty (20) days following delivery of a written request therefor by Indemnitee to the Corporation; and (ii) to Indemnitee Agent within twenty (20) days following the later of a written request therefor by Indemnitee Agent to the Corporation and determination by the Corporation to advance expenses to Indemnitee Agent pursuant to the Corporation's discretionary authority hereunder.

Section 6. NOTICE OF CLAIM. Indemnitee shall, as a condition precedent to his or her right to be indemnified under this Article VI, and Indemnitee Agent shall, as a condition precedent to his or her ability to be indemnified under this Article VI, give the Corporation notice in writing as soon as practicable of any claim made against Indemnitee or Indemnitee Agent, as the case may be, for which indemnification will or could be sought under this Article VI. Notice to the Corporation shall be directed to the secretary of the Corporation at the principal business office of the Corporation (or such other address as the Corporation shall designate in writing to Indemnitee). In addition, Indemnitee or Indemnitee Agent shall give the Corporation such information and cooperation as it may reasonably require and as shall be within Indemnitee's or Indemnitee Agent's power.

Section 7. ENFORCEMENT RIGHTS. Any indemnification provided for in Sections 1 or 2 or 3 shall be made no later than sixty (60) days after receipt of the written request of Indemnitee. If a claim or request under this Article VI, under any statute, or under any provision of the Corporation's Articles of

Incorporation providing for indemnification is not paid by the Corporation, or on its behalf, within sixty (60) days after written request for payment thereof has been received by the Corporation, Indemnitee may, but need not, at any time thereafter bring suit against the Corporation to recover the unpaid amount of the claim or request, and subject to Section 19, Indemnitee shall also be entitled to be paid for the expenses (including attorneys' fees) of bringing such action. It shall be a defense to any such action (other than an action brought to enforce a claim for expenses incurred in connection with any action, suit or proceeding in advance of its final disposition) that Indemnitee has not met the standards of conduct which make it permissible under applicable law for the Corporation to indemnify Indemnitee for the amount claimed, but the burden of proving such defense shall be on the Corporation, and Indemnitee shall be entitled to receive interim payments of expenses pursuant to Section 5 unless and until such defense may be finally adjudicated by court order or judgment for which no further right of appeal exists. The parties hereto intend that if the Corporation contests Indemnitee's right to indemnification, the question of Indemnitee's right to indemnification shall be a decision for the court, and no presumption regarding whether the applicable standard has been met will arise based on any determination or lack of determination of such by the Corporation (including its Board or any subgroup thereof, independent legal counsel or its shareholders). The Board of Directors may, in its discretion, provide by resolution for similar or identical enforcement rights for any Indemnitee Agent.

Section 8. ASSUMPTION OF DEFENSE. In the event the Corporation shall be obligated to pay the expenses of any proceeding against the Indemnitee (or Indemnitee Agent), the Corporation, if appropriate, shall be entitled to assume the defense of such proceeding with counsel approved by Indemnitee (or Indemnitee Agent), which approval shall not be unreasonably withheld, upon the delivery to Indemnitee (or Indemnitee Agent) of written notice of its election so to do. After delivery of such notice, approval of such counsel by Indemnitee (or Indemnitee Agent) and the retention of such counsel by the Corporation, the Corporation will not be liable to Indemnitee (or Indemnitee Agent) under this Article VI for any fees of counsel subsequently incurred by Indemnitee (or Indemnitee Agent) with respect to the same proceeding, unless (i) the employment of counsel by Indemnitee (or Indemnitee Agent) is authorized by the Corporation, (ii) Indemnitee (or Indemnitee Agent) shall have reasonably concluded that there may be a conflict of interest of such counsel retained by the Corporation between the Corporation and Indemnitee (or Indemnitee Agent) in the conduct of such defense, or (iii) the Corporation ceases or terminates the employment of such counsel with respect to the defense of such proceeding, in any of which events then the fees and expenses of Indemnitee's (or Indemnitee Agent's) counsel shall be at the expense of the Corporation. At all times, Indemnitee (or Indemnitee Agent) shall have the right to employ other counsel in any such proceeding at Indemnitee's (or Indemnitee Agent's) expense.

Section 9. APPROVAL OF EXPENSES. No expenses for which indemnity shall be sought under this Article VI, other than those in respect of judgments and verdicts actually rendered, shall be incurred without the prior consent of the Corporation, which consent shall not be unreasonably withheld.

Section 10. SUBROGATION. In the event of payment under this Article VI, the Corporation shall be subrogated to the extent of such payment to all of the rights of recovery of the Indemnitee (or Indemnitee Agent), who shall do all things that may be necessary to secure such rights, including the execution of such documents necessary to enable the Corporation effectively to bring suit to enforce such rights.

Section 11. EXCEPTIONS. Notwithstanding any other provision herein to the contrary, the Corporation shall not be obligated pursuant to this Article VI:

1.   Excluded Acts. To indemnify Indemnitee (i) as to circumstances in which indemnity is expressly prohibited pursuant to California law, or (ii) for any acts or omissions or transactions from which a director may not be relieved of liability pursuant to California law; or

2.   Claims Initiated by Indemnitee. To indemnify or advance expenses to Indemnitee with respect to proceedings or claims initiated or brought voluntarily by Indemnitee and not by way of defense, except with respect to proceedings brought to establish or enforce a right to indemnification under this Article VI or any other statute or law or as otherwise required under the California General Corporation Law, but such indemnification or advancement of expenses may be provided by the Corporation in specific cases if the Board of Directors has approved the initiation or bringing of such suit; or

3.   Lack of Good Faith. To indemnify Indemnitee for any expenses incurred by the Indemnitee with respect to any proceeding instituted by Indemnitee to enforce or interpret this Article VI, if a court of competent jurisdiction determines that such proceeding was not made in good faith or was frivolous; or

Section 12. PARTIAL INDEMNIFICATION. If Indemnitee is entitled under any provision of this Article VI to indemnification by the Corporation for some or a portion of the expenses, judgments, fines or penalties actually or reasonably incurred by the Indemnitee in the investigation, defense, appeal or settlement of any civil or criminal action, suit or proceeding, but not, however, for the total amount thereof, the Corporation shall nevertheless indemnify Indemnitee for the portion of such expenses, judgments, fines or penalties to which Indemnitee is entitled.

Section 13. COVERAGE. This Article VI shall, to the extent permitted by law, apply to acts or omissions of (i) Indemnitee which occurred prior to the adoption of this Article VI if Indemnitee was a director or officer of the Corporation or was serving at the request of the Corporation as a director or officer of another Corporation, partnership, joint venture, trust or other enterprise, at the time such act or omission occurred; and (ii) Indemnitee Agent which occurred prior to the adoption of this Article VI if Indemnitee Agent was an employee or other agent of the Corporation or was serving at the request of the Corporation as an employee or agent of another Corporation, partnership, joint venture, trust or other enterprise at the time such act or omission occurred. All rights to indemnification under this Article VI shall be deemed to be provided by a contract between the Corporation and the Indemnitee in which the Corporation hereby agrees to indemnify Indemnitee to the fullest extent permitted by law, notwithstanding that such indemnification is not specifically authorized by the Corporation's Articles of Incorporation, these Bylaws or by statute. Any repeal or modification of these Bylaws, the California General Corporation Law or any other applicable law shall not affect any rights or obligations then existing under this Article VI. The provisions of this Article VI shall continue as to Indemnitee and Indemnitee Agent for any action taken or not taken while serving in an indemnified capacity even though the Indemnitee or Indemnitee Agent may have ceased to serve in such capacity at the time of any action, suit or other covered proceeding. This Article VI shall be binding upon the Corporation and its successors and assigns and shall inure to the benefit of Indemnitee and Indemnitee Agent and Indemnitee's and Indemnitee Agent's estate, heirs, legal representatives and assigns.

Section 14. NON-EXCLUSIVITY. Nothing herein shall be deemed to diminish or otherwise restrict any rights to which Indemnitee or Indemnitee Agent may be entitled under the Corporation's Articles of Incorporation, these Bylaws, any agreement, any vote of shareholders or disinterested directors, or under the laws of the State of California.

Section 15. SEVERABILITY. Nothing in this Article VI is intended to require or shall be construed as requiring the Corporation to do or fail to do any act in violation of applicable law. If this Article VI or any portion hereof shall be invalidated on any ground by any court of competent jurisdiction, then the Corporation shall nevertheless indemnify Indemnitee or Indemnitee Agent to the fullest extent permitted by any applicable portion of this Article VI that shall not have been invalidated.

Section 16. MUTUAL ACKNOWLEDGMENT. Both the Corporation and Indemnitee acknowledge that in certain instances, Federal law or applicable public policy may prohibit the Corporation from indemnifying its directors and officers under this Article VI or otherwise. Indemnitee understands and acknowledges that the Corporation has undertaken or may be required in the future to undertake with the Securities and Exchange Commission to submit the question of indemnification to a court in certain circumstances for a determination of the Corporation's right under public policy to indemnify Indemnitee.

Section 17. OFFICER AND DIRECTOR LIABILITY INSURANCE. The Corporation shall, from time to time, make the good faith determination whether or not it is practicable for the Corporation to obtain and maintain a policy or policies of insurance with reputable insurance companies providing the officers and directors of the Corporation with coverage for losses from wrongful acts, or to ensure the Corporation's performance of its indemnification obligations under this Article VI. Among other considerations, the Corporation will weigh the costs of obtaining such insurance coverage against the protection afforded by such coverage. Notwithstanding the foregoing, the Corporation shall have no obligation to obtain or maintain such insurance if the Corporation determines in good faith that such insurance is not reasonably available, if the premium costs for such insurance are disproportionate to the amount of coverage provided, if the coverage provided by such insurance is limited by exclusions so as to provide an insufficient benefit, or if Indemnitee is covered by similar insurance maintained by a subsidiary or parent of the Corporation.

Section 18. NOTICE TO INSURERS. If, at the time of the receipt of a notice of a claim pursuant to Section 6 hereof, the Corporation has director and officer liability insurance in effect, the Corporation shall give prompt notice of the commencement of such proceeding to the insurers in accordance with the procedures set forth in the respective policies. The Corporation shall thereafter take all necessary or desirable action to cause such insurers to pay, on behalf of the Indemnitee, all amounts payable as a result of such proceeding in accordance with the terms of such policies.

Section 19. ATTORNEYS' FEES. In the event that any action is instituted by Indemnitee under this Article VI to enforce or interpret any of the terms hereof, Indemnitee shall be entitled to be paid all court costs and expenses, including reasonable attorneys' fees, incurred by Indemnitee with respect to such action, unless as a part of such action, the court of competent jurisdiction determines that the action was not instituted in good faith or was frivolous. In the event of an action instituted by or in the name of the Corporation under this Article VI, or to enforce or interpret any of the terms of this Article VI, Indemnitee shall be entitled to be paid all court costs and expenses, including attorneys' fees, incurred by Indemnitee in defense of such action (including with respect to Indemnitee's counterclaims and crossclaims made in such action), unless as a part of such action the court determines that Indemnitee's defenses to such action were not made in good faith or were frivolous. The Board of Directors may, in its discretion, provide by resolution for payment of such attorneys' fees to any Indemnitee Agent.

Section 20. NOTICE. All notices, requests, demands and other communications under this Article VI shall be in writing and shall be deemed duly given (i) if delivered by hand and receipted for by the addressee, on the date of such receipt, or (ii) if mailed by domestic certified or registered mail with postage prepaid, on the third business day after the date postmarked.

ARTICLE VII.

RECORDS AND REPORTS

Section 1. MAINTENANCE AND INSPECTION OF SHARE REGISTER. The Corporation shall keep at its principal executive office, or at the office of its transfer agent or registrar, if either be appointed and as determined by resolution of the Board of Directors, a record of its shareholders, giving the names and addresses of all shareholders and the number and class of shares held by each shareholder.

A shareholder or shareholders of the Corporation holding at least five percent (5%) in the aggregate of the outstanding voting shares of the Corporation may (i) inspect and copy the records of shareholders' names and addresses and shareholdings during usual business hours upon five days prior written demand upon the Corporation, and/or (ii) obtain from the transfer agent of the Corporation, upon written demand and upon the tender of such transfer agent's usual charges for such list, a list of the shareholders' names and addresses, who are entitled to vote for the election of directors, and their shareholdings, as of the most recent record date for which such list has been compiled or as of a date specified by the shareholder subsequent to the date of demand. Such list shall be made available by the transfer agent on or before the later of five (5) days after the demand is received or the date specified therein as the date as of which the list is to be compiled. The record of shareholders shall also be open to inspection upon the written demand of any shareholder or holder of a voting trust certificate, at any time during usual business hours, for a purpose reasonably related to such holder's interests as a shareholder or as the holder of a voting trust certificate. Any inspection and copying under this Section may be made in person or by an agent or attorney of the shareholder or holder of a voting trust certificate making such demand.

Section 2. MAINTENANCE AND INSPECTION OF BYLAWS. The Corporation shall keep at its principal executive office, or if its principal executive office is not in the State of California at its principal business office in this state, the original or a copy of the Bylaws as amended to date, which shall be open to inspection by the shareholders at all reasonable times during office hours. If the principal executive office of the Corporation is outside this State and the Corporation has no principal business office in this state, the Secretary shall, upon the written request of any shareholder, furnish to such shareholder a copy of the Bylaws as amended to date.

Section 3. MAINTENANCE AND INSPECTION OF OTHER CORPORATE RECORDS. The accounting books and records and minutes of proceedings of the shareholders and the Board of Directors and any committee or committees of the Board of Directors shall be kept at such place or places designated by the Board of Directors, or, in the absence of such designation, at the principal executive office of the Corporation. The minutes shall be kept in written form and the accounting books and records shall be kept either in written form or in any other form capable of being converted into written form. Such minutes and accounting books and records shall be open to inspection upon the written demand of any shareholder or holder of a voting trust certificate, at any reasonable time during usual business hours, for a purpose reasonably related to such holder's interests as a shareholder or as the holder of a voting trust certificate. Such inspection may be made in person or by an agent or attorney, and shall include the right to copy and make extracts. The foregoing rights of inspection shall extend to the records of each subsidiary of the Corporation.

Section 4. INSPECTION BY DIRECTORS. Every director shall have the absolute right at any reasonable time to inspect all books, records, and documents of every kind and the physical properties of the Corporation and each of its subsidiary Corporations. This inspection by a director may be made in person or by an agent or attorney and the right of inspection includes the right to copy and make extracts of documents.

Section 5. ANNUAL REPORT TO SHAREHOLDERS. The annual report to shareholders referred to in Section 1501 of the General Corporation Law is expressly dispensed with, but nothing herein shall be interpreted as prohibiting the Board of Directors from issuing annual or other periodic reports to the shareholders of the Corporation as they deem appropriate.

Section 6. FINANCIAL STATEMENTS. A copy of any annual financial statement and any income statement of the Corporation for each quarterly period of each fiscal year, and any accompanying balance sheet of the Corporation as of the end of each such period, that has been prepared by the Corporation shall be kept on file in the principal executive office of the Corporation for twelve (12) months and each such statement shall be exhibited at all reasonable times to any shareholder demanding an examination of any such statement or a copy shall be mailed to any such shareholder.

If no annual report for the last fiscal year has been sent to shareholders, the Corporation shall, upon the written request of any shareholder made more than 120 days after the close of such fiscal year, deliver or mail to such shareholder, within thirty (30) days after such request a balance sheet as of the end of such fiscal year and an income statement and statement of changes in financial position for such fiscal year.

If a shareholder or shareholders holding at least five percent (5%) of the outstanding shares of any class of stock of the Corporation make a written request to the Corporation for an income statement of the Corporation for the three-month, six-month or nine-month period of the then current fiscal year ended more than thirty (30) days prior to the date of the request and a balance sheet of the Corporation as of the end of such period and, in addition, if no annual report for the last fiscal year has been sent to shareholders, a balance sheet as of the end of such fiscal year and an income statement and statement of changes in financial position for such fiscal year, then, the chief financial officer shall cause such statements to be prepared, if not already prepared, and shall deliver personally or mail such statement or statements to the person making the request within thirty (30) days after the receipt of such request.

The income statements and balance sheets referred to in this section shall be accompanied by the report thereon, if any, of any independent accountants engaged by the Corporation or the certificate of an authorized officer of the Corporation that such financial statements were prepared without audit from the books and records of the Corporation.

Section 7. ANNUAL STATEMENT OF GENERAL INFORMATION. The Corporation shall file annually with the Secretary of State of the State of California, on the prescribed form, a statement setting forth the names and complete business or residence addresses of all incumbent directors, the number of vacancies on the Board of Directors, if any, the names and complete business or residence addresses of the chief executive officer, secretary and chief financial officer, the street address of its principal executive office or principal business office in this state and the general type of business constituting the principal business activity of the Corporation, together with a designation of the agent of the Corporation for the purpose of service of process, all in compliance with Section 1502 of the Corporations Code of California.

ARTICLE VIII.

GENERAL CORPORATE MATTERS

Section 1.   RECORD DATE FOR PURPOSES OTHER THAN NOTICE AND VOTING. For purposes of determining the shareholders entitled to receive payment of any dividend or other distribution or allotment of any rights or entitled to exercise any rights in respect of any other lawful action (other than action by shareholders by written consent without a meeting), the Board of Directors may fix, in advance, a record date, which shall not be more than sixty (60) days prior to any such action, and in such case only shareholders of record on the date so fixed are entitled to receive the dividend, distribution or allotment of rights or to exercise the rights, as the case may be, notwithstanding any transfer of any shares on the books of the Corporation after the record date fixed as aforesaid, except as otherwise provided in the California General Corporation Law.

If the Board of Directors does not so fix a record date, the record date for determining shareholders for any such purpose shall be at the close of business on the day on which the board adopts the resolution relating thereto, or the sixtieth (60th) day prior to the date of such action, whichever is later.

Section 2.   CHECKS,   DRAFTS,   EVIDENCES   OF INDEBTEDNESS. All checks, drafts or other orders for payment of money, notes or other evidences of indebtedness, issued in the name of or payable to the Corporation, shall be signed or endorsed by such person or persons and in such manner as, from time to time, shall be determined by resolution of the Board of Directors.

Section 3.   CORPORATE CONTRACTS AND INSTRUMENTS; HOW EXECUTED. The Board of Directors, except as otherwise provided in these bylaws, may authorize any officer or officers, agent or agents, to enter into any contract or execute any instrument in the name of and on behalf of the Corporation, and such authority may be general or confined to specific instances; and, unless so authorized or ratified by the Board of Directors or within the agency power of an officer, no officer, agent or employee shall have any power or authority to bind the Corporation by any contract or engagement or to pledge its credit or to render it liable for any purpose or for any amount.

Section 4.   CERTIFICATES FOR SHARES.   A certificate or certificates for shares of the capital stock of the Corporation shall be issued to each shareholder when any such shares are fully paid, and the Board of Directors may authorize the issuance of certificates for shares as partly paid provided that such certificates shall state the amount of the consideration to be paid therefor and the amount paid thereon. All certificates shall be signed in the name of the Corporation by the chairman of the board or vice chairman of the board or the president or a vice president and by the chief financial officer or an assistant chief financial officer or the secretary or any assistant secretary, certifying the number of shares and the class or series of shares owned by the shareholder. Any or all of the signatures on the certificate may be facsimile. In case any officer, transfer agent or registrar who has signed or whose facsimile signature has been placed upon a certificate shall have ceased to be such officer, transfer agent or registrar before such certificate is issued, it may be issued by the Corporation with the same effect as if such person were an officer, transfer agent or registrar at the date of issue.

Section 5.   LOST CERTIFICATES. Except as hereinafter in this Section provided, no new certificates for shares shall be issued in lieu of an old certificate unless the latter is surrendered to the Corporation and cancelled at the same time. The Board of Directors may in case any share certificate or certificate for any other security is lost, stolen or destroyed, authorize the issuance of a new certificate in lieu thereof, upon such terms and conditions as the board may require including provision for indemnification of the Corporation secured by a bond or other adequate security sufficient to protect the Corporation against any claim that may be made against it, including any expense or liability, on account of the alleged loss, theft or destruction of such certificate or the issuance of such new certificate.

Section 6.   REPRESENTATION OF SHARES OF OTHER CORPORATIONS. The chairman of the board, the president, or any vice president, or any other person authorized by resolution of the Board of Directors by any of the foregoing designated officers, is authorized to vote on behalf of the Corporation any and all shares of any other Corporation or Corporations, foreign or domestic, standing in the name of the Corporation. The authority herein granted to said officers to vote or represent on behalf of the Corporation any and all shares held by the Corporation in any other Corporation or Corporations may be exercised by any such officer in person or by any person authorized to do so by proxy duly executed by said officer.

Section 7.   CONSTRUCTION AND DEFINITIONS. Unless the context requires otherwise, the general provisions, rules of construction, and definitions in the California General Corporation Law shall govern the construction of these Bylaws. Without limiting the generality of the foregoing, the singular number includes the plural, the plural number includes the singular, and the term "person" includes both a Corporation and a natural person.

ARTICLE IX.

AMENDMENTS

Section 1.   AMENDMENT BY SHAREHOLDERS. New Bylaws may be adopted or these Bylaws may be amended or repealed by the vote or written consent of holders of a majority of the outstanding shares entitled to vote; provided, however, that if the articles of incorporation of the Corporation set forth the number of authorized directors of the Corporation, the authorized number of directors may be changed only by an amendment of the Articles of Incorporation.

Section 2.   AMENDMENT BY DIRECTORS. Subject to the rights of the shareholders as provided in Section 1 of this Article IX, Bylaws, other than a Bylaw or an amendment thereof changing the authorized number of directors, may be adopted, amended or repealed by the Board of Directors.

THE ISSUANCE OF STOCK

It is important to know that the issuance of stock in a corporation is the issuance of a "security" under both federal and state securities laws. The issuance of a security which is either not registered, nor exempt from the federal and/or state securities laws, is a crime. It is important to comply with both federal and state securities laws and determine if the sale of the stock falls into an exemption under either federal or state law. There are several federal and California state exemptions which are available to a corporate issuer. You should consult with an attorney on this matter.

It is also important to note that in certain situations a gift of stock will be made to another by the person who purchases or receives the stock. In this event, the person receiving the stock as a gift will not be a party to the original representations made at the time as to the use of the stock by the purchaser. These representations are usually required for exemption purposes. It is, therefore, handy to have the person who receives the stock as a gift sign a receipt for stock. It is also important to have the original purchaser complete a Subscription Agreement and Purchaser Questionnaire. These two forms comply with the issuance of stock under a federal exemption known as Regulation D and a California exemption under either Section 25102(f) or 25102(h) of the California securities laws. An exemption under Regulation D requires that a Form D be filed with the Securities and Exchange Commission and a n exemption under both sections 25102(f) and (h) require a from be filed with the California Securities Commissioner. Please consult an attorney for the preparation of these two forms. In addition, since the securities laws are frequently changed please verify the accuracy of the information in both the Subscription Agreement and Purchaser Questionnaire before you use them.

SAMPLE

PURCHASER QUESTIONNAIRE

ALL INFORMATION WILL BE TREATED CONFIDENTIALLY

Gentlemen:

The undersigned has expressed an interest in purchasing shares of common stock (the "Stock") in _____, a California corporation (the "Company") pursuant to an investor disclosure letter, dated April ___, 1989 (the "Letter"). I understand that the Stock is being offered and sold by the Company pursuant to exemptions from registration for a private placement of securities under the Securities Act of 1933, as amended (the "Act"), and similar exemptions under applicable state laws. The undersigned is furnishing, and understands that the Company will be relying upon, the information contained herein in order to enable the Company to verify that the undersigned meets the investor suitability standards and to insure that the requirements of such exemptions are satisfied.

1.   Please initial in the appropriate space next to the representations set forth below:

_____ I have such knowledge and experience in financial and business matters that I am capable of evaluating the merits and risks of an investment in the Stock of the Company and I have had the opportunity to consult with my financial, business or legal advisor in evaluating the merits and risks of an investment in the Company. I am offering as evidence of my knowledge and experience in these matters the information provided below.

_____ I represent that I have adequate means for providing for my needs on a current basis, have no need for liquidity in this investment and I am able to bear the economic risk of an investment in the Stock of the size contemplated. In making this statement, I have considered whether I could afford to hold the Stock for an indefinite period and bear a total loss of this investment. I offer as evidence of my ability to bear the economic risk the information set forth below.

_____ Any purchase of the Stock will be solely for my own account, and not for the account of any other person or with a view to any resale or distribution thereof, whether in whole or in part.

Please answer all questions fully.

1. Name of Investor:_____

2. Residence Address and telephone number: _____
_____

3. My social security number is: _____

4. My annual income (without including the income of my spouse unless he or she is a co-investor) is:

Year	Gross Income
1987	$ _____
1988	$ _____
1989 (estimated)	$ _____

5. My net worth is in excess of:

____ $200,000   ____ $500,000

____ $750,000   ____ $1,000,000

6. Business and Financial Knowledge:

6.1   Please describe your educational background, including degrees obtained:_____

_____

_____

6.2 Please describe your present occupation, and the positions you have held and the nature of such positions within the last five years:_____

_____

_____

7. Investment Experience:

7.1   Please indicate the frequency of your investment in securities:

____ Often ____ Occasionally ____ Seldom____ Never

7.2 Please indicate whether you make your own investment decisions:

____ Always ____ Frequently   ____ Usually____ Rarely

7.3 How many years of experience do you have with start-up hightechnologycompanies?_____

8. Information re status as a suitable investor:

I am an "accredited investor" and "not counted purchaser" because I am (check any applicable boxes):

____ A natural person whose individual net worth, or joint net worth with the undersigned's spouse, exceeds $1,000,000.

____ A natural person who had an individual income in excess of $200,00 in each of the two most recent years and reasonably expects an income in excess of $200,000 in the current year; or a combined income with his or her spouse in excess of $300,000 in each of the two most recent years and reasonably expects an income in excess of $300,000 in the current year.

I understand that the Company will be relying on the accuracy and completeness of my responses to the foregoing questions and I represent and warrant to the Company as follows:

(i) The answers to the above questions are complete and correct and may be relied upon by the Company in determining whether the sale of Stock for which I have executed this Purchaser Questionnaire is exempt from registration under the Securities Act of 1933 and qualification under applicable state securities laws.

           (ii)   I will notify the Company immediately of any material change in any statement made herein occurring prior to the issuance of any Stock to the undersigned.

_____

Name (Please Print)

_____

Date

_____

Signature

_____

Name (Please Print)

_____

Date

_____

Signature

SAMPLE

SUBSCRIPTION AGREEMENT

THE SECURITIES REFERRED TO HEREIN HAVE NOT BEEN REGISTERED UNDER THE SECURITIES ACT OF 1933, AS AMENDED NOR QUALIFIED UNDER ANY STATE SECURITIES LAWS IN RELIANCE UPON EXEMPTIONS THEREFROM. THE SECURITIES MAY BE ACQUIRED FOR INVESTMENT PURPOSES ONLY AND NOT WITH A VIEW TO DISTRIBUTION OR RESALE, AND MAY NOT BE SOLD, MORTGAGED, PLEDGED, HYPOTHECATED OR OTHERWISE TRANSFERRED OR OFFERED TO BE SO TRANSFERRED WITHOUT AN EFFECTIVE REGISTRATION STATEMENT FOR SUCH SECURITIES UNDER THE SECURITIES ACT OF 1933 AND QUALIFICATION UNDER APPLICABLE STATE SECURITIES LAWS, OR AN OPINION OF COUNSEL SATISFACTORY TO THE COMPANY THAT SUCH TRANSACTION SHALL NOT VIOLATE ANY FEDERAL OR STATE SECURITIES LAWS.

_____,Inc.,
a California corporation

SUBSCRIPTION AGREEMENT

1.　　Subscription. The undersigned ("Subscriber") hereby irrevocably agrees to purchase on the terms and conditions described herein and in the private placement memorandum dated _____, 19__ (the "Memorandum") which accompanies this Subscription

Agreement, the number of shares of stock (the "Stock") in _____Inc., a California corporation (the "Company") set forth opposite the Subscriber's signature below, at a purchase price of $____ per share.

2.   <u>Purchase Price</u>. The purchase price per share is $____, which is payable in full by delivery herewith of a check made payable to "_____."

3.   <u>Representations of Subscriber</u>. The Subscriber hereby represents and warrants that:

(a)   The Subscriber is capable of bearing the high economic risks of this investment, including the possible loss of the entire investment;

(b)   The Stock is being acquired for a long term investment only and for the Subscriber's own account and not with a view to, or for sale in connection with, the distribution thereof, nor with any present intention of distributing or selling the Stock.

(c)   The Subscriber understands that the Stock has **not** been qualified under the California Corporate Securities Law of 1968 or any other applicable state securities laws and that the Stock has **not** been registered under the Securities Act of 1933, as amended (the "Act"), and are being offered and sold pursuant to exemptions thereunder, and that in this connection the Company is relying on the Subscriber's representations set forth in this Subscription Agreement and in the Subscriber's Purchaser Questionnaire;

(d)   The Subscriber understands and agrees that: the Stock many not be offered or transferred in any manner unless (i) subsequently registered under the Act, or (ii) an opinion of counsel satisfactory to the Company has been rendered stating that such offer or transfer will not violate any federal or state securities laws, or (iii) such sale is made in compliance with all of the requirements of Rule 144 promulgated by the Securities and Exchange Commission under the Act;

(e)   The information which the Subscriber provided in Subscriber's Purchaser Questionnaire is true and correct on the date hereof and the representations contained therein are hereby confirmed; should any such information change prior to the issuance of Stock to Subscriber, Subscriber agrees to immediately provide the Company with a written notice setting forth the corrected information;

(f)   By executing this Subscription Agreement, the Subscriber hereby acknowledges receipt of the Memorandum, including the Company's financial statements, attached thereto as Appendix A.;

(g)   The Subscriber has been furnished with the materials relating to the Company, the offering of the Stock, or anything set forth in the Memorandum, which they have requested, and have been afforded the opportunity to make inquiries of and have received answers from the officers and directors of the Company concerning the Company and such matters, and have further been afforded the opportunity to obtain any additional information necessary to verify the information set forth in the Memorandum (to the extent the Company possess such information or could acquire it without unreasonable effort or expense);

(h)   The Subscriber has substantial means of providing for his or her current needs and personal contingencies and has no need for liquidity in this investment;

(i)   The Subscriber has determined that the Stock is a suitable investment for him or her and that he or she could bear a complete loss of his or her investment;

(j) The Subscriber has relied on his or her own tax and legal advisor and his or her own investment counselor with respect to the investment considerations of purchasing the Stock in the Company;

(k) The Subscriber is aware that the Company may sell the Stock to him or her only if he or she qualifies according to the express standards stated herein. The Subscriber represents and warrants that he or she meet the following investment standards:

(i) The Subscriber is a citizen of the United States of America and is at least 21 years of age.

(ii)(A) The Subscriber meets one of the standards of an "Accredited Investor," as such term is defined in Rule 501(a) of Regulation D promulgated under the Act and one of the standards of a "Not Counted Purchaser" as such term is defined in Rule 260.102.13 of the Rules of the California Commissioner of Corporations, as indicated in the Subscriber's Purchaser Questionnaire; OR

(ii)(B) The Subscriber has (x) individual income of more than $200,000 (exclusive of any income attributable to his or her spouse) or joint income with his or her spouse of more than $200,000 in each of the two last years with an expectation of achieving the same income in this year, or (y) an individual or combined net worth, including home and personal property, in excess of $1,000,000.

(l) The Subscriber has not been furnished with any offering literature other than the Memorandum, and did not learn of the offering described therein through any general advertising or other literature, and he or she has relied only on the information obtained in the Memorandum and the information furnished or made available to them by the Company described in subparagraph 3(g) above;

(m) Subscriber has been furnished and has carefully read the Memorandum, including the documents and other materials which are appendices thereto or otherwise supplied to him or her;

(n) No representations or warranties have been made to the Subscriber by the Company or any persons acting on behalf of the Company, or any affiliate of them, other than the representations set forth herein and in the Memorandum; and

(o) The foregoing representations, warranties and agreements of the Subscriber shall survive the sale and issuance of the Stock to the Subscriber.

4. <u>Acceptance</u>. Subscriber hereby confirms his or her understanding that the Company has full and absolute discretion to accept or reject this subscription in whole. In the case of rejection of this subscription, the total subscription funds of the Subscriber will be promptly returned to him or her.

5. <u>Changes in Subscriber Information</u>. If there are any changes in any information supplied in your Purchaser Questionnaire, please list such changes.

_____

_____

_____

6.   <u>Ownership of Stock</u>. Please print the name and address of the name of the individual(s) which will own the Stock.

(1) Name

_____

First   Middle   Last

_____

Street Address

_____

City   State   Zip Code

Social Security No.

_____

(1) Name

_____

First   Middle   Last

_____

Street Address

_____

City   State   Zip Code

Social Security No.

_____

Number of shares subscribed for at $_____ per share: _____shares

7.   <u>Title to Stock</u>. Please indicate by check mark below the manner in which title to the Stock will be held.

____ Community Property ____ Joint Tenancy

____ Tenancy in Common ____ Single Person

____ Separate Property   ____ Other (please indicate)

8.   <u>Signature</u>. Each person in whose name the Stock is to be issued must sign in the space below.

IN WITNESS WHEREOF, the undersigned(s) executes and agrees to be bound by this Subscription Agreement.

Dated this _____ day of _____, 1989.

_____
Number of Shares Subscribed for

_____
Print Name of Individual

_____
Signature

_____
Print Name of Individual

_____
Signature

MINUTES

Once the Bylaws have been written, they must be adopted. The incorporator can adopt the Bylaws, issue stock to the shareholders and resign as incorporator. An incorporator's primary role is to incorporate the corporation. After this task has been completed it is customary for the incorporator to resign. The incorporator's resignation, adoption of the bylaws and the issuance of stock should be evidenced in the organizational minutes, i.e., the first minutes, of the corporation.

Minutes are written documents which evidence the corporation's intent as well as its course of action. Once the incorporator resigns, the shareholders will elect the Board of Directors who will, in turn, elect the officers of the corporation.

The organizational minutes usually set forth such items as the corporation's principal place of business, its accounting year, bank, issuance of stock, election of directors, and other preliminary business information. Each major transaction, for example, the lease of real property, the purchase of major computer equipment, the corporation's entering into contracts such as employment agreements, should be evidenced by resolutions set forth in the corporation's minutes.

Normally, Bylaws provide that action by either, the shareholders or directors may be taken at a meeting or by written consent. If action is taken by written consent, then the resolutions, embodied in the minutes must be signed by those who may vote and those whose signatures, in the aggregate, satisfy the percentage required for that action (i.e., a majority or 50%).

The Small Business Form Book

SAMPLE

RECEIPT FOR STOCK TRANSFERRED AS A GIFT

I, _____, hereby acknowledge that I have received as a gift for no consideration and for my own purposes not to be distributed, assigned or resold to others, Stock Certificate No. ___, which is restricted stock subject to both federal and California State law legend restrictions, for _____ shares of the common stock of _____, Incorporated, a California corporation.

Dated:_____, 19__.

By : _____
    Stock Recipient

SAMPLE

ORGANIZATIONAL MINUTES

UNANIMOUS WRITTEN CONSENT OF THE SHAREHOLDERS OF

_____

_____, 19__

The undersigned, being all of the shareholders of _____ Inc., a California corporation, do hereby, jointly and severally pursuant to Section 603(a) of the California Corporations Code, authorize the adoption of the following resolutions, and any and all actions contemplated thereby:

1. <u>Election of Directors</u>.

      RESOLVED: That the following persons are elected as directors of this Corporation:

_____

_____

_____

IN WITNESS WHEREOF, the undersigned have set their hands hereto on _____ _____, 19__.

_____   _____
Shareholder   Shareholder

_____
Shareholder

SAMPLE

UNANIMOUS WRITTEN CONSENT OF THE
BOARD OF DIRECTORS OF

_____

_____, 19__

The undersigned, being all of the directors of _____ _____ Inc., a California corporation, do hereby, jointly and severally pursuant to Section 307(c) of the California Corporations Code, authorize the adoption of the following resolutions, and any and all actions contemplated thereby:

    1. <u>Resignation of Incorporator</u>.

        The undersigned, _____, resigns as the incorporator of the Corporation.

_____

Incorporator

    2. <u>Bylaws</u>.

        RESOLVED: That the Corporation's Bylaws as presented   to the incorporator are hereby ratified approved and adopted as the Bylaws of this Corporation.

    3. <u>Election of Officers</u>.

        RESOLVED: That the following persons are elected as officers of this Corporation:

President   _____

Vice President   _____

Secretary   _____

Chief Financial Officer   _____

4. <u>Principal Office</u>.

     RESOLVED: That the principal executive office of the Corporation is hereby fixed at _____, California.

5. <u>Corporate Seal and Minute Book</u>.

     RESOLVED: That a form of Corporate Seal consisting of two concentric circles with the name of the Corporation in one circle and the words and figures "Incorporated _____" and "California" in the other is hereby adopted as the seal of this Corporation, and the Secretary of this Corporation is directed to place an impression thereof in the margin following this resolution.

6. <u>Stock Certificate</u>.

     RESOLVED: That the form of stock certificate representing the stock of the Corporation attached hereto as "Exhibit "A" is adopted for use by this Corporation to represent shares of common capital stock of this Corporation.

7. <u>Accounting Year; Accountant</u>.

     RESOLVED: That this Corporation hereby adopts a calendar accounting year ending December 31 each year.

RESOLVED FURTHER: That _____ is hereby appointed as the accountants for the Corporation.

8. Bank Account.

RESOLVED: That the officers of this Corporation be and they hereby are authorized and directed to open a bank account or accounts with _____ and that checks on the account or accounts be signed by the President, Vice President, Chief Financial Officer, or Secretary.

RESOLVED FURTHER: That the officers of this Corporation be and they hereby are authorized and directed to execute and deliver those documents, including signature cards, which may be required to open the account or accounts.

9. Officers Authorized to Contract.

RESOLVED: That the President, Vice President, Chief Financial Officer, or Secretary any of them, be and the same hereby are, authorized to sign contacts and obligations of the Corporation in the ordinary course of its business; provided that no contract or obligation involving the transfer of any substantial right in any major asset of the Corporation shall be so signed and no substantial indebtedness shall be incurred without prior approval of the Board of Directors or any Committee thereof duly authorized to give such approval.

10. Share Certificate.

RESOLVED: That the minute book established by the Incorporator be and hereby is adopted as the form of minute book of this Corporation.

WHEREAS: This Corporation is authorized to issue an aggregate of _____ shares of its common capital stock without par value, and none of said shares has been issued; and

WHEREAS: This Corporation intends to issue _____ _____ of such shares for cash;

RESOLVED: That the Corporation sell and issue an aggregate of not to exceed _____ shares of its common capital stock without par value to the following named persons for cash, at the price of $_____ per share in accordance with the terms of the California Corporate Securities Law of 1968 and pursuant to the Rules and Regulations pertaining to that Law, in particular Rules 260.102.6 and 260.102.8:

Name	Number of Shares	Consideration
_____	_____	$_____
_____	_____	_____

RESOLVED FURTHER: That the shares of voting common stock authorized at this meeting to be sold and issued by this Corporation shall be offered and sold strictly in accordance with the terms of the exemption from qualification provided for in Section 25102(f) of the California Corporations Code, so that counsel for this Corporation will be in a position to sign and file with the California Commissioner of Corporations the form of notice specified in that Section.

RESOLVED FURTHER: That _____, as counsel for the Corporation, prepare the necessary notice to the Commissioner of Corporations pursuant to Subdivision (f) of Section 25102 of the California Corporations Code, such notice to be executed by the President of the Corporation.

RESOLVED FURTHER: That the officers of this Corporation be and they hereby are authorized and directed to execute all documents and to take such action as they may deem necessary or advisable to carry out and perform the purposes of these resolutions.

11. Subchapter "S" Election.

WHEREAS: This Corporation qualified as a "small business corporation" within the meaning of Section 1371(a) of the Internal Revenue Code of 1954, as amended; and

WHEREAS: This Corporation and its proposed shareholders intend to elect "Subchapter S" tax treatment as an "electing small business corporation" in accordance with Sections 1371(b) and 1372 of the Code;

RESOLVED: That this Corporation hereby elects to be treated as a "small business corporation" for income tax purposes under those provisions of the Code.

RESOLVED FURTHER: That the officers of this Corporation be and they hereby are authorized and directed, jointly and severally, to obtain the consent of the shareholders to the foregoing election and to do any and all things and to execute and deliver any and all correct forms and other documents and file some with the Internal Revenue Service which they deem necessary or appropriate to effectuate the "Subchapter S" election for this Corporation.

12. Licenses and Permits.

RESOLVED: That the officers of this Corporation be and hereby are authorized and directed to take necessary actions to obtain any licenses and permits necessary to the business of this Corporation.

13. Organizational Expenses.

RESOLVED: That the President, Secretary, or Chief Financial Officer of this Corporation be and they hereby are authorized and directed to pay the expenses of incorporation and organization of this Corporation.

IN WITNESS WHEREOF, the undersigned have set their hands hereto on _____, 19__.

_____
Director

_____
Director

_____
Director

RESOLUTIONS

The Board of Directors is responsible for managing the affairs of the corporation. Material decisions made by the Board of Directors should be memorialized in the form of a resolution. A resolution is a formal expression of the will or opinion of an official body adopted by a vote. Generally, matters raised before the board are first "moved" and "seconded," then discussed and, finally, put to a vote.

Some of the key maintenance actions which should be documented with a regularly drafted, approved, and reported resolution include: election of corporation officers (Corporations Code Section 312); adoption, amendment, or repeal of bylaws (Corporations Code Section 211); election of directors to fill vacancies of the board (Corporations Code Section 305 (a)); designation of committees of the Board of Directors and allocation of authority to them (Corporations Code Sections 307 and 311); calling of shareholders' meetings (Corporations Code Section 600); and the amendment of Articles of Incorporation (Corporations Code Sections 212(a), 901-902, 2302, and 2304).

Specific actions concerning insurance and indemnity should also be documented by resolution. You should include a resolution which reflects the approval of indemnification of corporate officers, directors, and agents (Corporation Code Section 317 (e)).

Any major business transaction should be reflected in the minute book by resolution. Consider the following list: approval of issuance and sale of corporate securities (Corporations Code Section 409); declaration of dividends and other distributions, and share repurchases or redemptions (Corporations Code Sections 116, 300, and 311(f); approval of the sale, lease, conveyance, exchange, transfer or other dispositions of corporate property and assets (Corporations Code Sections 300 and 1001); approval of mergers and reorganizations (Corporations Code Sections 1101 and 1200); approval of adoption of pension, profit-sharing, and other employee benefit plans (Corporations Code Sections 207(f), 300, 315(b), and 408); approval of corporate borrowing and lending (Corporations Code Sections 207(g), 300, 310, 315-316, and 1501); authorization of choice of banks and signatures (Corporations Code Sections 313 and 315); and adoption of business policies and plans (Corporations Code Sections 300 and 311).

A resolution does not have to be drafted at a formal meeting. A resolution can be drafted by the attorney and then presented to each director of the corporation for signature. When resolutions are drafted and presented in this way, it is necessary that there be a unanimous written consent.

The format of most resolutions is simple. Generally, a resolution will begin with a citation to a section from the Corporations Code which gives the corporation the authority to draft the resolution. Next, it briefly describes the subject matter of the resolution and the purpose of its adoption. The "resolved" portion of the resolution basically affirms the directors' intent to adopt the resolution. Finally, the directors witness the resolution by signature.

The format of the resolution is not as important as the content. The resolution must contain language describing the transaction contemplated by the directors and evidence their approval. Some commonly used resolutions follow.

Resolutions which are incorporated into the minutes of a corporation are often attested to by the Corporation's secretary. The secretary's attestation is in the form of a Certificate of Secretary. A sample of which follows.

The sample resolutions below pertain to resolutions which have been adopted by the Board of Directors to enter into various agreements. The resolutions also state who has the authority to sign the agreements on behalf of the corporation.

SAMPLE

UNANIMOUS WRITTEN CONSENT
OF THE BOARD OF DIRECTORS
IN LIEU OF AN ANNUAL MEETING
OF
_____, INC.,
a California corporation

Date

Pursuant to the provisions of Section 307 of the Corporations Code of the State of California, the undersigned, constituting all of the Directors of _____, Inc., do hereby dispense with the formality of an annual meeting of Directors and do hereby adopt the following resolutions:

1. <u>Ratification of Acts of Directors</u>

RESOLVED: That all purchases, contracts, contributions, compensations and acts by the officers of the corporation since the last annual meeting of the Board be, and the same hereby are ratified and confirmed.

2. <u>Election of Officers</u>

RESOLVED: That the following persons be, and they hereby are,, elected as officers of this corporation for the ensuing year or until their successors are elected:

_____ President

_____ Secretary

_____ Chief Financial Officer

In witness whereof the following have set their hand hereto this __ day of ___, 19__.

_____
Director

_____
Director

_____
Director

SAMPLE

UNANIMOUS WRITTEN CONSENT OF THE
SHAREHOLDERS
IN LIEU OF ANNUAL MEETING
OF
_____, INC.
a California corporation

Date

Pursuant to the provisions of Section 603(a) of the Corporations Code of the State of California, the undersigned do hereby dispense with the formality of an annual meeting of Shareholders and hereby adopt the following resolutions:

1. <u>Ratification of Acts of Board of Directors</u>

RESOLVED: That all purchases, contracts, contributions, compensations, acts, proceedings, elections and appointments by the Board of Directors since the last annual meeting thereof and all acts of the Directors thereof for said period be, and the same hereby are, ratified and confirmed.

2. <u>Election of Directors</u>

RESOLVED: That the following persons be, and they hereby are, elected as Directors of this corporation for the ensuing year or until their successors are elected:

_____
Director

_____
Director

_____
Director

This consent shall be filed with the Secretary of this corporation, who is hereby instructed to insert it in the Minute Book for the corporation.

Dated:_____

_____
Shareholder

_____
Shareholder

_____
Shareholder

SAMPLE

UNANIMOUS WRITTEN CONSENT OF THE
BOARD OF DIRECTORS OF
_____, INC.
a California Corporation

Date

The undersigned, being all of the directors of _____, Inc., a California corporation, do hereby, jointly and severally pursuant to Section 307(b) of the California Corporations Code, authorize the adoption of the following resolutions, and any and all actions contemplated thereby:

1. <u>Issuance of Stock</u>

RESOLVED: That the Corporation shall issue to _____, a shareholder in the Corporation, a total of _____ shares in the Corporation.

IN WITNESS WHEREOF, the undersigned have set their hands hereto on (date).

_____
Director

_____
Director

_____
Director

SAMPLE

UNANIMOUS WRITTEN CONSENT OF THE
BOARD OF DIRECTORS OF
_____, INC.
a California Corporation

Date

The undersigned, being all of the directors of _____, Inc., a California corporation, do hereby, jointly and severally pursuant to Section 307(b) of the California Corporations Code, authorize the adoption of the following resolutions, and any and all actions contemplated thereby:

1. Limited Transferability of Stock

WHEREAS, the Shares being offered have limited transferability, therefore be it:

RESOLVED: That   the   Offering   of _____(date) is being made in reliance upon an exemption from the registration requirements of the Securities Act of 1933 and an exemption from the qualification requirements of the California Corporate Securities Act of 1968, and no public or other market will develop for the Shares as a result of this offering; and

RESOLVED FURTHER: That the transfer of Shares will not be transferrable without consent of the Corporation and none of the Corporation's Stock may be sold, transferred, assigned or otherwise disposed of by any shareholder, unless such Stock is registered under relevant federal and state securities laws or an exemption from such registration is demonstrated.

2. <u>Issuance of Stock</u>

RESOLVED: That the Corporation shall issue to
_____, a director and shareholder of the
Corporation, a total of _____ shares in the Corporation.

3. <u>Issuance of Stock</u>

RESOLVED: That the Corporation shall issue to
_____, a director and shareholder of the
Corporation, a total of _____ shares in the Corporation.

IN WITNESS WHEREOF the undersigned have set their
names hereto on _____(date).

_____
Director

_____
Director

_____
Director

SAMPLE

**UNANIMOUS WRITTEN CONSENT OF THE
BOARD OF DIRECTORS OF
_____, INC.
a California Corporation**

Date

The undersigned, being all of the directors of _____, Inc, a California corporation, do hereby, jointly and severally pursuant to Section 307(b) of the California Corporations Code, authorize the adoption of the following resolutions, and any and all actions contemplated thereby:

1. <u>Corporate Lease</u>

WHEREAS, this Corporation requires additional space for conducting business, and

WHEREAS, _____ (the "Lessor") agrees to lease to the Corporation the (description of premises, for example office space, storage space etc.), situated in the County of _____ in the State of _____, and described as (street address and city) for the monthly payments of $_____ commencing on _____ and ending on _____, and

WHEREAS, the Board of Directors deems it advisable that the Corporation lease said premises for _____(state purpose of premises) from Lessor for the aforementioned price; therefore, be it

RESOLVED: That the Corporation lease from the Lessor the aforesaid premises;

AND IT IS FURTHER RESOLVED: That the President of the Corporation, _____, is hereby authorized to enter into an agreement in behalf of this Corporation with said Lessor for the monthly payments of $_____, in advance on the first day of each month of the term beginning _____ and ending _____;

AND IT IS FURTHER RESOLVED: That the President of this Corporation is authorized to execute all instruments and make all payments necessary for the transfer and conveyance of this Corporation of the aforesaid building.

IN WITNESS WHEREOF, the undersigned have set their hands hereto on (date).

_____
Director

_____
Director

_____
Director

SAMPLE

UNANIMOUS WRITTEN CONSENT OF THE
BOARD OF DIRECTORS OF
_____, INC.
a California Corporation

Date

The undersigned, being all of the directors of _____, Inc., a California corporation, do hereby, jointly and severally pursuant to Section 307(b) of the California Corporations Code, authorize the adoption of the following resolutions, and any and all actions contemplated thereby:

1. <u>Corporation Contract</u>

WHEREAS, the Corporation has entered into a contract with _____ (name of company) for the purpose of providing _____ (description of service); and

WHEREAS, the contract is in all respects just and reasonable as to the Corporation at this time in that _____ (terms of payment), therefore be it:

RESOLVED: That the Corporation has entered into such contract with (name of corporation) and the directors of the Corporation have authorized and directed its execution on behalf of and as the act of the Corporation.

IN WITNESS WHEREOF, the undersigned have set their hands hereto on _____ (date)

_____
Director

_____
Director

_____
Director

SAMPLE

**UNANIMOUS WRITTEN CONSENT OF THE
BOARD OF DIRECTORS OF
_____, INC.
a California Corporation**

Date

The undersigned, being all of the directors of _____, Inc., a California corporation, do hereby, jointly and severally pursuant to Section 307(b) of the California Corporations Code, authorize the adoption of the following resolutions, and any and all actions contemplated thereby:

1. <u>Corporate Loan</u>

WHEREAS, the Corporation has determined it to be in the best interest of the Corporation to obtain a loan;

RESOLVED: the Corporation has entered into a Loan Agreement with the _____ (name of bank) (the "Agreement") on _____ (date), extending a line of credit to the Corporation in the amount of _____ (amount), and pursuant to the terms of the Agreement;

IN WITNESS WHEREOF, the undersigned have set their hands hereto on _____ (date).

_____
Director

_____
Director

_____
Director

SAMPLE

**UNANIMOUS WRITTEN CONSENT OF THE
BOARD OF DIRECTORS OF
_____, INC.
a California Corporation**

Date

The undersigned, being all of the directors of _____ Inc., a California corporation, do hereby, jointly and severally pursuant to Section 307(b) of the California Corporations Code, authorize the adoption of the following resolutions, and any and all actions contemplated thereby:

1. Employment Agreement

WHEREAS, the Corporation deems it to be in the Corporation's best interest to employ _____ as the Corporation's _____(job title);

RESOLVED: That in order to retain the services of _____ (name of employee) as _____ (job title) and to insure continuity of management for the Corporation, the Corporation is directed to execute a written contract of employment with _____ (name of employee) made for a term set forth in Article __ of the Employment Agreement ("Agreement") as _____ (job title) of the Corporation on the terms, and conditions and for the compensation set forth in the Agreement, a copy of which the Secretary is directed to make a part of the corporate records.

IN WITNESS WHEREOF, the undersigned have set their hands hereto on (date)

_____
Director

_____
Director

_____
Director

SAMPLE

CERTIFICATE OF SECRETARY

I hereby certify that the following is a true and correct copy of the Resolutions Adopted by Unanimous Written Consent of the Board of Directors of_____, Inc., a California corporation on _____, 198_, and that the foregoing have not been changed and remain in full force and effect.

WHEREAS, it is deemed to be in the best interest of the Company to enter into a _____ Agreement dated _____, 198_ by and between the Company and _____, and all agreements contemplated thereby and a _____ Agreement (collectively the "Agreements") (which are attached hereto), for the purpose of _____.

NOW, THEREFORE, BE IT RESOLVED, that _____, _____, _____, or any of them, acting alone, be, and they hereby are, authorized and directed to execute and deliver the Agreements; and

RESOLVED FURTHER, that each person who, as an officer or representative of the Company has the authority to sign the Agreements and any other document delivered in connection with the transaction described in the _____ Agreement was, is and will be at the respective times of such signing and delivery, a duly elected or appointed and qualified officer or representative of the Company.

RESOLVED FURTHER, that any of the above individuals be, and they hereby are, authorized and directed to take any and all additional action and to execute such other documents as are deemed necessary or appropriate in order to carry out the intent of the Agreement.

Secretary _____

SHAREHOLDERS' AGREEMENT

A shareholders agreement is an agreement between a corporation's shareholders which regulates one or more aspects of the corporation's structure and management. A shareholders agreement is not required by law, but it is an effective means of defining and enforcing the expectations of the shareholders. Members of a closely held corporation, usually small in number, often draft a shareholders agreement because they have a great personal interest in the structure and management of the business.

The main reason shareholders draft a shareholders agreement is to limit or place restrictions on how stock can be transferred. Generally, this right to restrict the transfer of shares can be defined and redefined, so long as it is first authorized in the corporation's Articles of Incorporation.

A shareholders agreement contains many general provisions as well. For example, a shareholders agreement will state the amount of shares issued, to whom, and the consideration tendered. It will also include provisions concerning officer responsibilities and conduct.

Provisions concerning officer responsibilities and conduct should state who has access to what, under what circumstances a member should be dismissed, and specific voting requirements. These provisions should also address specific situations such as who can sign checks and for what amount and who has access to corporate documents. Most of these provisions are "boiler plate," or standard provisions, and should be drafted to reflect the specific intent of the shareholders.

The following sample shareholders agreement sets forth most of these major provisions. This sample will give you a starting point at which to ask or present to your fellow shareholders the terms of transfer.

Perhaps the most significant provision in the shareholders agreement is the buy-sell agreement. A buy-sell provision establishes who can buy a shareholder's stock. It usually requires the seller to first obtain written consent from the other shareholders. This provision essentially sets forth the terms allowing the other shareholders or the corporation to purchase the stock of the withdrawing, retiring, or deceased shareholder. It also specifies the terms of the offer, include time limits for acceptance and price.

There are four basic buy-sell agreements: (i) mandatory agreement; (ii) option with the remaining shareholders or the corporation; (iii) option with the seller; and (iv) right of first refusal. Of course, many shareholders agreements contain provisions regarding each of these.

Under a mandatory agreement, the remaining shareholders or the corporation is required to purchase the stock of the withdrawing or deceased shareholder.

Under the second buy-sell agreement, either the shareholders or the corporation is allowed to exercise the option of purchasing the stock of the withdrawing or deceased shareholder. Because the transfer of shares ultimately changes the structure of management, it is very important to include specific provisions regarding voting rights.

In an agreement with an option with the seller, the estate of the withdrawing or deceased shareholder may elect to sell the stock to the remaining shareholder or the corporation, in which case they would be required to purchase.

The fourth type of buy-sell agreement, the right of first refusal, requires the seller to offer his stock to the remaining shareholder or corporation, who then have the option to buy if they so choose. Under an agreement where the corporation exercises its option to buy the stock, the agreement is called a "stock repurchase." Corporations Code Section 500 sets forth financial standards which apply to this purchase. Often, funds come from profits or insurance policies. Where the shareholders purchase the stock, the plan is called a "cross Purchase." In a cross purchase, purchasing shareholders buy the shares with their personal funds or from insurance policies which they have taken out on each other. If neither the remaining shraeholders nor the corporation opt to purchase the shares, a clause should be included which provides for a public sale.

A shareholders agreement is an excellent way to protect members in the event of a shareholder's withdrawal, death, retirement, or disability. Whether or not you decide to adopt a shareholders agreement, it is beneficial to discuss it with an attorney. Drafting such an agreement may seem unnecessary, because the provisions are often future oriented, but for many small closely held corporations, it is good insurance. The agreement can of course be changed to reflect new limits and include new provisions which may be necessary.

Having discussed and decided on how and under what conditions the corporation can effect stock transfers will save an enormous amount of time spent with an attorney. Advance preparation will allow an attorney to more quickly draft your agreement without spending unnecessary time explaining issues you have already decided.

SAMPLE

**SHAREHOLDERS' AGREEMENT
OF**

A California Corporation

This Shareholders' Agreement (the "Agreement") is entered into on this _____ day of November, 1989, by and among _____, an individual ("_____") and _____, an individual ("_____"), (collectively the "Shareholders" and individually a "Shareholder") and _____, Inc., a California corporation ("_____" or the "Corporation"), all of whom are sometimes hereinafter referred to collectively as the "Parties" and all individually as a "Party".

<u>RECITALS</u>

A.   The Corporation is authorized to issue _____ (_____) shares of Common Stock (the "Shares"), of which _____ thousand shares are issued to the Shareholders.

B. With respect to all of the Shares, the Parties desire to promote their mutual interests by making certain agreements and imposing certain restrictions and obligations on the Shareholders, the Corporation, and on the Shares and any additional shares issued by the Corporation, which agreements will affect all shares of the Corporation owned or required now and hereafter by the Shareholders.

C. With respect to the Parties hereto, the Shareholders desire to impose certain restrictions and obligations as to the ownership interest of each Shareholder and any parent thereof and agree to be bound specifically by the terms as set forth in Article IX hereof.

D.   The Parties desire to provide that in the event the Corporation desires to issue additional shares, that a right of first refusal be granted to the Shareholders to purchase such shares.

E.   The Parties to this Agreement desire to provide that in the event any of the Shareholders desire to sell all or any part of its Shares, a right of first refusal is to be granted first to the remaining Shareholders and then to the Corporation to purchase such Shares.

Now, therefore, in consideration of the mutual covenants, duties, obligations and conditions contained herein, he parties agree as follows:

ARTICLE I
DESIGNATION OF SHAREHOLDERS

The Corporation is incorporated under the laws of the State of California, and the Corporation has issued, for good and valuable consideration, _____ Shares of its _____ authorized Shares to the Shareholders as follows:

_____   _____ Shares

_____   _____ Shares

ARTICLE II
CONTINUATION OF AGREEMENT

The Corporation shall not transfer or issue additional Shares to a new shareholder who does not become a party to this Agreement.

ARTICLE III
ARTICLES OF INCORPORATION AND BYLAWS

The Shareholders agree that the Articles of Incorporation and Bylaws of the Corporation, attached hereto as Exhibit A, are and shall remain the Articles of Incorporation and Bylaws of the Corporation unless required to be amended in order to be consistent with the provisions of this Shareholders' Agreement.

ARTICLE IV
VOTING OF SHARES

4.1 <u>Voting</u>. Except as otherwise set forth in this Agreement, each Shareholder shall be entitled to cast one vote for each Share held by him.

4.2 <u>Intent of Agreement</u>. Each of the Shareholders shall vote or cause to be voted its Shares held of record or owned beneficially by such Shareholder in such a manner as will carry out the intent and purpose of, and cause the effectuation and implementation of all the covenants contained in this Agreement.

4.3 <u>Voting Requirements</u>. The consent of the majority in interest of Shareholders shall be required to approve any of the following acts:

(a) Amendment or repeal or alteration in any way of any provision of the Articles of Incorporation or Bylaws of the Corporation;

(b) Merger or consolidation of the Corporation; or

(c) Transfer of all or substantially all of the assets of the Corporation.

ARTICLE V
OFFICERS

5.1 <u>Designation of Officers</u>. Subject to the provisions of this Agreement, the Shareholders agree that the selected Board of Directors shall appoint the officers in the Corporation.

5.2 <u>Duties and Responsibilities of Officers</u>. The duties and responsibilities of the officers of the Corporation shall be as set forth in the Bylaws or as otherwise approved by a majority in interest of the Shareholders.

5.3 <u>Salaries of Officers</u>. Salaries of the officers shall be determined by the Board of Directors.

5.4 <u>Termination of an Officer or Director</u>. Notwithstanding the provisions of Section 303 of the California Corporations Code, which, to the extent they are inconsistent With the provisions hereof, are expressly waived, or any provision hereof, any person elected by a Shareholder or appointed by a director, may be terminated as an officer or director upon the occurrence of an event as set forth below ("Terminating Event"), provided that such Terminating Event is properly set forth in a written notice prepared by a Shareholder and delivered to the officer or director within ten days after the Shareholder learns of the Terminating Event:

(a) Engaged in misconduct or a willful breach of his Agreement of such a nature as to render such Shareholder's continued presence as an officer or director personally or professionally obnoxious or detrimental to the other Shareholders;

(b) Been convicted by final action of any court of any offense punishable as a felony involving moral turpitude;

(c) Made an assignment for the benefit of the Creditors or been declared, or has filed a petition seeking to be declared a bankrupt;

(d) Been declared to be insane, or incompetent to manage such Shareholder's affairs; or

(e) Caused the Corporation to be convicted of a crime or to incur criminal penalties in material amounts.

5.5 <u>The Event of Termination</u>. In the event of any such termination, the person terminated as an officer agrees to sell any Share ownership he/she has in the Corporation to the other Shareholders, and the other Shareholders agree to purchase any such Shares then owned by the terminated officer pursuant to the terms set forth herein in Article X.

ARTICLE VI
MANAGEMENT AND CONTROL

6.1 <u>Board of Directors</u>. The Board shall initially consist of ____ members who shall be elected annually by the Shareholders at a meeting called for that purpose. The Board of Directors shall conduct the affairs of the Corporation pursuant to the terms of the Bylaws of the Corporation.

6.2 <u>Voting</u>. The Board of Directors shall vote on all issues as required and each Director shall be entitled to one vote. A majority vote of the Board of Directors shall be sufficient and binding for Board action.

6.3 <u>Employment of President</u>. _____ shall be employed by the Corporation as the President. Such employment shall be pursuant to an employment agreement and shall remain effective pursuant to its terms.

6.4 <u>Employment of Chief Financial Officer</u>. _____
shall be employed by the Corporation as the Chief Financial Officer.
Such employment shall be pursuant to an employment agreement and
shall remain effective pursuant to its terms.

6.5 <u>Conduct of Business</u>. The Shareholders agree to use
their best efforts to cause the business to be conducted in accordance
with sound business practices, in a lawful manner, and to endeavor to
preserve the goodwill of the Corporation's Suppliers, customers,
employees, and others having business relations with it.

ARTICLE VII
BOOKS. RECORDS, AND REPORTS

The Shareholders shall cause the Corporation to
maintain the books, records and other documents required by Section
1500 of the California Corporations Code.

ARTICLE VIII
SHAREHOLDERS' PARTICIPATION

Each Shareholder shall devote time and attention to
the business of the Corporation, sufficient to perform its obligations
pursuant to the terms hereof or the Bylaws.

ARTICLE IX
RIGHT OF FIRST REFUSAL

In the event that the Board of Directors of the Corporation
decides to issue further Shares of the Corporation's stock, such Shares
shall be issued in equal amounts to each Shareholder unless otherwise

agreed between them. The Shares so issued shall be issued at such price and upon such terms and conditions as the Board of Directors shall determine.

ARTICLE X
BUY-SELL RESTRICTIONS

10.1 <u>Restriction Against Transfer</u>. After the date of execution of this Agreement, each Shareholder agrees that it will not transfer, assign, hypothecate or in any way alienate any of its Shares, or any right or interest therein, whether voluntary or by operation of law, without the prior written consent of the Corporation and the other Shareholder. Any purported transfer and violation of any provision of this Agreement shall be void and ineffectual, shall not operate to transfer any interest or title in the purposed transferee and shall give the other Shareholder and the Corporation an option to purchase such Shares in the manner and on the terms and conditions provided for herein.

10.2 <u>Requirement of Offer</u>. By executing this Agreement each Shareholder grants to the other Shareholder and to the Corporation, the first right to acquire all Shares which a Shareholder desires to alienate. In the event that any shareholder (the "Disposing Shareholder") should desire to sell, assign or otherwise transfer or dispose of its Shares during its existence, it shall first give written notice, by registered or certified mail, to the Secretary of the Corporation and to the remaining Shareholder of the Corporation (the "Remaining Shareholder") of its intention to do so.

10.3 <u>Notice of Offer</u>. The notice of an offer ("Notice") shall state:

(1) The name of the proposed transferee;

(2) The number of Shares proposed to be transferred.

(3) The price per share;
(4) The terms of payment; and

(5) The address of the Disposing Shareholder.

Promptly on receipt of the Notice, the secretary shall notify the directors, and within ten (10) days, meeting of the Corporation's Board of Directors shall be duly lad, noticed, and held for the purpose of considering the proposed transfer.

10.4 <u>Acceptance by Shareholders</u>.   The Remaining Shareholder shall have the first option to purchase all (and not less than all) of the Disposing Shareholder's Shares owned by the Remaining Shareholder at the date Notice is given, at the price and on the terms stated in the Notice. The Remaining Shareholder shall be deemed to have timely exercised this option if Notice of its acceptance of the offer is received, before midnight of the fifteenth (15th) day following the date of receipt of the Notice, and is either: (i) delivered to the Disposing Shareholder in person; or (ii) sent by registered or certified mail to the address of the Disposing Shareholder set forth in the Notice. If the Remaining Shareholder elects to exercise its option, the purchase shall be consummated within ten (10) days after all necessary corporate action has been taken by the Remaining Shareholder. The Remaining Shareholder covenant to use its best efforts to promptly obtain such approvals and to promptly take such action.

10.5 <u>Acceptance by Corporation</u>. If the option is not exercised by the Remaining Shareholder as to all Shares set forth in the Notice within the fifteen-day period, notice of the proposed transfer shall then be given by registered mail to the Corporation, which shall have the option to purchase all the Shares (and not less than all) not purchased by the Remaining Shareholder at the price and on the same terms and conditions specified in the Notice. Within ten (10) days after the mailing of the Notice, the Corporation shall deliver to the Secretary of the Corporation a written Notice to purchase the Shares and such purchase of the Shares shall be consummated within ten (10) days thereafter.

The right of the Corporation to exercise the option and to purchase the stock is subject to the restrictions governing the right of a corporation to purchase its own stock contained in Chapter 5 of the California Corporations Code, and such other pertinent governmental restrictions as are now, or my hereafter become, effective.

10.6 <u>Acceptance by Transferee</u>.   If the Remaining Shareholder or the Corporation do not exercise their options to purchase all of the Disposing Shareholder's shares, then the Disposing Shareholder shall have the right to sell its Shares offered to the transferee set forth in the Disposing Shareholder's original notice, provided that such sale is consummated within fifteen (15) days after expiration of the applicable option periods and on the same terms and conditions as set forth in the Disposing Shareholder's original notice, and provided, further, that such transferee agrees to be bound by the terms and conditions of this Agreement and executes this Agreement or amendment thereto reflecting such obligations.

10.7 <u>Purchase Price</u>. The purchase price for each of the Shares transferred pursuant to the provisions of this Agreement shall be determined as follows:

(a) Unless and until changed as provided in subparagraph (b) or (c) of this Article, the purchase price for each Share is fixed at the book value, as readjusted annually pursuant to subparagraph (b) below, or the price per Share as set forth in the Notice, whichever is less.

(b) Within 30 days of December 31 of each year hereafter, the Shareholders shall review the financial condition of the Company as of the end of the preceding calendar year and shall determine by mutual agreement the book value of the Corporation, which, if agreed on, shall be the value of the Corporation until a different book value is agreed on or otherwise established under the provisions of this Agreement. If the Shareholders are unable to mutually agree on the fair market book value of the Corporation as provided above, any Shareholder may require that the book value of the Corporation be established by appraisal. In this event, the appraisal shall be conducted by an MAI appraiser, selected by a majority in interest of the Shareholders, and the cost of the appraisal shall be borne by the Corporation.

(c) If the Shareholders do not mutually agree on a new book value for the Corporation, and if no Shareholder requests an appraisal under the provisions of subparagraph (b) of this Article within sixty (60) days after the 31st of December on which the book value was to be determined, the book value established during the preceding year shall be effective for the balance of that year and until December 31 of the succeeding year, when the Shareholders shall again endeavor to determine a new book value by mutual agreement. Any book value agreed on or otherwise established under the foregoing provisions shall be retroactively adjusted for any dividend or other distribution to Shareholders declared after the determination of the book value of the Corporation.

10.8 <u>Payment of Purchase Price</u>. The purchase price for each of the Shares sold pursuant to this Agreement shall be paid in cash at the time of closing the sale.

10.9   Shares Involuntarily Transferred.

(a) The Option. The Shareholders first and then the Corporation shall have the option to purchase any Shares acquired under judicial order, legal process, execution, attachment, enforcement of a pledge, trust or encumbrance, or sale under any of them, or in any manner not a voluntary act by the Shareholders.

(b) Purchase Price. The purchase price to the Shareholders or the Corporation for the Shares referred to in subparagraph (a) herein shall be the price per share paid by the transferee of the Shares involuntarily transferred.

(c) Payment of Purchase Price. Upon the determination of the purchase price referred to in subparagraph (b) herein, the Shareholders or the Corporation shall pay for the Shares in cash.

10.10 Place and Time of Closing. If an offer is accepted, the sale shall be closed at the principal office of the Corporation at a time determined by the Corporation, which time shall be during the Corporation's ordinary business hours and shall be not less than thirty (30) nor more than forty-five (45) days after the day on which the notice of acceptance is delivered. The closing shall be at the price and on the terms determined pursuant to this Agreement.

10.11 Delivery of Shares and Documents. Upon the closing of a sale the purchasing Shareholder or the Corporation hall deliver to the Disposing Shareholder cash as provided for in this Agreement and the Disposing Shareholder shall deliver to the Purchasing Shareholder the certificates evidencing the Shares being sold, and such assignments, consents to transfer, and other documents as may be required by counsel for the corporation.

ARTICLE XI
BUY-SELL UPON OTHER EVENTS

In the event ("Terminating Event") a Shareholder:

(1) Attempts in any manner whatsoever to dissolve the Corporation without the consent of all Shareholders subject to this Agreement; or

(2) Is adjudicated bankrupt (voluntary or involuntary) or insolvent, or makes an assignment for the benefit of his creditors; The Remaining Shareholder shall be given the first option for a period of thirty (30) days following notice of any such Terminating Event to purchase all or any portion of the shares owned by such Shareholder ("Terminated Shares"). Notice shall be given to such Shareholder ("Terminated Shareholder") and/or his/her legal representative stating the intention of the Remaining Shareholder to purchase the Terminated Shares. In the event the Remaining Shareholder does not elect to purchase all of the Terminated Shares, the Corporation shell be entitled to purchase the remainder of the Terminated Shares upon the same terms and conditions applicable to the Remaining Shareholder, provided, however, that the rights of the Corporation to exercise such option shall be subject to the laws of the State of California governing the rights of a corporation to purchase to own shares. The purchase price and terms of payment shall be determined on the date of the Terminating Event in accordance with the book value of the Shares at the time of the declaration of insolvency of the Terminated Shareholder or the filing of a petition of bankruptcy (whether voluntary or involuntary) by the Terminated Shareholder or a creditor thereof. In the event a Shareholder is declared insolvent or adjudicated bankrupt by any court or regulatory body, the insolvent or bankrupt Shareholder's voting rights shall transfer (the "Transferred Shares") to the solvent Shareholder and

such Shareholder shall have the right to vote such Transferred Shares until such time as the insolvent or bankrupt Shareholder is declared solvent or discharged from bankruptcy, unless such Transferred Shares have been sold pursuant to the provisions herein.

ARTICLE XII
RESTRICTIONS ON CERTIFICATES

The Corporation and each Shareholder agrees that all certificates representing all of the Shares which at any time are subject to the provisions of this Agreement shall have endorsed upon them the following legend:

"The shares represented by this certificate are subject to certain restrictions against transfer under the terms of an agreement entered into by this corporation's shareholders, a copy of which is on file at the principal office of this corporation. All terms and conditions of said agreement are hereby incorporated by reference and made a part of this certificate."

Under no circumstances shall any sale or other transfer of any of the Shares subject hereto be valid until the proposed transferee thereof shall have executed and become a party to his Agreement and thereby shall have become subject to the Provisions hereof, unless the requirements of same are waived by written consent of the Corporation and all of the Shareholders. The Corporation agrees that it will not issue additional shares until the purchaser of such Shares shall have executed and become a party to this Agreement.

ARTICLE XIII
TERMINATION OF AGREEMENT

This Agreement shall terminate and the certificates representing the Shares subject to this Agreement shall be released from the terms of this Agreement on the occurrence of any of the following events:

(a) Cessation of the business of the Corporation;

(b) Written agreement of all of the Shareholders then bound by the terms of this Agreement; or

(c) Bankruptcy, receivership or dissolution of the Corporation.

Upon termination of this Agreement for any of the above reasons, the certificates for the Shares held by each Shareholder shall be surrendered to the Corporation and the Corporation shall issue new certificates for the same number of Shares, but without endorsement required by this Agreement.

ARTICLE XIV
MERGER. CONSOLIDATION. ETC.

Notwithstanding any provision of this Agreement which may be or may appear to be to the contrary, in the event that the Corporation shall (i) merge or consolidate with any other corporation, or (ii) sell, transfer or otherwise dispose of all or a substantial part of its assets, or (iii) issue for consideration, authorized and unissued Shares of stock of the corporation (all of which actions are hereinafter referred to in this Section as a "Transaction") and the acquire in such Transaction being hereinafter referred to as a "Purchaser" and such Transaction has been approved by a vote of the shareholders of the Corporation representing not less than ninety percent (90%) of the issued and outstanding Shares of he Corporation and the Purchaser, as a condition of the Transaction, required the purchase of all or any portion of the hares issued to the Shareholder (the Shareholders, the Shareholders' spouses, any representatives and any transferee, distributees or other successors-in-interest, as the case may be, being hereinafter referred to in this Section as Shareholders"), then the

Shareholders each agree for the benefit of the Corporation to sell to the Purchaser all or a proportionate amount of Shares (such proportionate amount to be in the same ratios as the ratios of Shares owned as between themselves immediately prior to the Transaction). In such event the Shareholders shall be given written notice by the corporation of the terms and conditions of the Transaction and the identity of the Purchaser. The notice shall set forth the number of Shares of the Shareholders (all or a portion) to be acquired, the price, terms and conditions of such acquisition and the time, date and place of closing.

ARTICLE XV
GENERAL CLAUSES

15.1 <u>Governing Law and Jurisdiction</u>. This Agreement shall be governed by and interpreted in accordance with the laws of the State of California. Each of the parties hereto consents to the jurisdiction for the enforcement of this Agreement and matters pertaining to the transaction and activities contemplated hereby.

15.2 <u>Notices</u>. All notices and other communications provided for or permitted hereunder shall be made by hand delivery, first class mail, telex or telecopier, addressed as follows:

<u>PARTY</u>   <u>ADDRESS</u>

All such notices and communications shall be deemed to have been duly given: when delivered by hand, if personally delivered; three (3) business days after deposit in any United States Post Office in the Continental United States, postage prepaid, if mailed; when answered back, if telexed; and when receipt is acknowledged, if telecopied.

15.3 <u>Attorney's Fees</u>. In the event a dispute arises with respect to this Agreement, the party prevailing in such dispute shall be entitled to recover all expenses, including, without limitation, reasonable attorneys' fees and expenses, incurred in ascertaining such party's rights, in preparing to enforce, or in enforcing such party's rights under this Agreement, whether or not it was necessary for such party to institute suit.

15.4 <u>Complete Agreement Of The Parties</u>. This Agreement supersedes any and all other agreements, either oral or in writing, between the parties with respect to the subject matter hereof and contains all of the covenants and agreements between the parties with respect to such subject matter in any manner whatsoever. Each party to this Agreement acknowledges that no representations, inducements, promises or agreements, oral or otherwise, have been made by any party, or anyone herein, and that no other agreement, statement or promise not contained in this Agreement shall be valid or binding. This Agreement may be changed or amended only by an amendment in writing signed by all of the parties or their respective successors-in-interest.

15.5 <u>Binding</u>. This Agreement shall be binding upon and inure to the benefit of the successors-in-interest, assigns and personal representatives of the respective parties.

15.6 <u>Number and Gender</u>. Whenever the singular number is used in this Agreement and when required by the context, the same shall include the plural, end the masculine gender shall include the feminine and neuter genders and the word "person" shall include corporation, firm, partnership or other form of association.

15.7 <u>Failure To Object Not A Waive</u>. The failure of either party to this Agreement to object to, or to take affirmative action with respect to, any conduct of the other Which is in violation of the terms of this Agreement, shall not be construed as a waiver of the violation or breach or of any future violation, breach or wrongful conduct.

15.8 <u>Unenforceable Terms</u>. Any provision hereof prohibited by law or unenforceable under any applicable law of any jurisdiction shall as to such jurisdiction be ineffective without affecting any other provision of this Agreement. To the full extent, however, that the provisions of such applicable law may be waived, they are hereby waived to the end that this Agreement be deemed to be a valid and binding agreement enforceable in accordance with its terms.

15.9 <u>Execution In Counterparts</u>. This Agreement may be executed in several counterparts and when so executed shall constitute one agreement binding on all the parties, notwithstanding that all the parties are not signatory to the original and same counterpart.

15.10 <u>Further Assurance</u>. From time to time each party will execute and deliver such further instruments and will take such other action as any other party may reasonably request in order to discharge and perform their obligations and agreements hereunder and to give effect to the intentions expressed in this Agreement.

15.11 <u>Incorporation By Reference</u>. All exhibits referred to in this Agreement are incorporated herein in their entirety by such reference.

15.12 <u>Cross-References</u>. All cross-references in this agreement, unless specifically directed to another agreement or document, refer to provisions in this Agreement, and shall not be deemed to be references to the overall transaction or to any other agreements or documents.

15.13 <u>Miscellaneous Provisions</u>. The various headings nd numbers herein and the grouping of provisions of this Agreement into separate articles and paragraphs are for the purpose of convenience only and shall not be considered a part hereof. The language in all parts of this Agreement shall in all cases be construed in accordance to its fair meaning as if repaired by all parties to the Agreement and not strictly for or against any of the parties.

        IN WITNESS WHEREOF, this Agreement has been entered into as of the date first above written.

                    _____, Inc.
                    a California corporation

                    _____
                    By: _____, President

                    _____, an individual

                    _____
                    _____, an individual

CHAPTER TWO

CORPORATE MAINTENANCE

There are many formalities associated with the maintenance of a corporation. Corporations are statutory entities and must comply with state law if the are to remain in good standing. A corporation which is in good standing is one which has maintained good corporate records, held annual meetings for both the shareholders and the directors, filed federal and state tax forms, paid its annual fee to the California State Franchise Tax Board and filed its annual Statement by a Domestic Stock Corporation together with the appropriate fee with the California Secretary of State's office.

In addition, there may be a number of other forms which must be filed with federal and state regulatory agencies, licensing bureaus, and other organizations depending upon the corporation's business. These must not be overlooked and are an important part of corporate maintenance.

Corporate maintenance may include such items as the preparation of a resignation for an officer or director of the corporation. Two types of resignations are set forth below. The first is a simple resignation which is signed by the officer or director and placed in the minute book of the corporation. The second requires that the officer or director indemnify the corporation for any claims it may have in connection with the director's resignation or prior relationship with the corporation.

SAMPLE

SIMPLE RESIGNATION

The undersigned, _____, hereby tenders his resignation as a director and officer of _____, Inc., a California Corporation (the "Company"), effective immediately.

IN WITNESS WHEREOF, the undersigned has executed this Resignation effective as of the ____ day of _____, 198_.

_____

SAMPLE

RESIGNATION WITH INDEMNITY

The undersigned, _____, hereby tenders his resignation as a director and officer of _____, Inc., a _____ corporation (the "Company"), effective immediately.

In connection therewith, the undersigned, does hereby acknowledge and agree that he has no claims against the Company and further agrees to forever release the Company, its predecessors, assigns, agents, employees, attorneys and representatives from any and all causes of action in law or in equity of any kind whatsoever.

IN WITNESS WHEREOF, the undersigned has executed this Resignation effective as of the ____ day of ____, 198_.

_____

CHAPTER THREE

CORPORATE AND BUSINESS FORMS

The two most popular forms of business agreements for the start-up corporation are the employment agreement and the non-disclosure or confidentiality agreement. Employment agreements vary dramatically according to the particular facts of the potential relationship between the employer and employee and the position of the employee within the corporation. The following sample employment agreement is for use with the employment of a senior level executive or president in a small, closely-held corporation. Certain amenities are provided for the employee, such as insurance, transportation and moving allowances.

In most instances certain confidentiality provisions are contained directly in the employment agreement as in the example below. Therefore, a separate confidentiality agreement does not normally need to be signed by an employee who is subject to an employment agreement with such provisions. If, however, conversations between the corporation and the employee are to involve corporate secrets or confidential information prior to the employee's signing an employment agreement, then a confidentiality agreement should be signed before conversations begin. Additionally, a confidentiality agreement should be signed whenever the corporation is discussing its business with outside third parties and such discussions will involve sharing financial information or business information which is important to the corporation's development and operations.

Despite the infinite variety of employment relationships, any employment contract should contain certain basic terms. An employment contract should include the terms of employment, the general duties of the employee, the employee's compensation, and provisions for termination.

It is important to note that if an employment contract cannot be performed within one year from its making, the contract is invalid unless it, or a note or memorandum of it, is in writing and signed. An employment contract which gives an employee authority to enter into contracts on behalf of the corporation must also be in writing.

In addition to salary, the compensation provisions should specify whether any other benefits, such as commission, profit-sharing, insurance, retirement and disability, and stock options are available, and under what circumstances. Provisions also might be included to specify overtime pay, cost-of-living increases, pension plans and/or death benefits, vacation pay, and severance pay.

A stock option clause in an employment contract gives an employee an opportunity to purchase stock in the company at a certain price (or at a price computed pursuant to a specified formula as set forth in the agreement) during a specific time period. This option is contingent on continued employment, and is nonassignable, unlike some options which may be granted to third persons.

The termination provision of an employment contract is critical. It should be as specific as possible and attempt to anticipate the various situations that might arise. Aside from the right to terminate an employee upon a breach of duty, an employer may want to consider termination provisions based on an employee's inability to perform his or her duties, low profits, and major corporate reorganization.

The agreement should also include an arbitration provision in the event there is an objection to the termination. Arbitration is an arrangement where parties to a dispute choose and agree in advance to abide by an impartial third party's ruling rather than go through formal litigation. The contract should include a clause providing the employee with proper notice and an opportunity for objection. Finally, the company may want to include a clause which gives it the right to terminate the employee without cause.

In addition to these general provisions, the contract should include any provisions applicable to the particular employment situation. In the case of officers' duties, it is good practice to specify what actions cannot be done without consent of the board of directors. For example, a director who works as the company accountant or administrator may not be permitted to write checks or draw on certain accounts without the approval of the other directors. It is also a good idea to draft a bylaw provision or board resolution as to the employee's authority.

In any type of business, special consideration should be given to protect the corporation's trade secrets, customer lists, patented inventions, and processes. Generally, anything the employee acquires by virtue of, and within the scope and purpose of his or her employment belongs to the employer. This does not apply when an employee creates an invention, unless the employee was specifically hired to create the item. The employer does, however, have the "shop right" to free use and duplication of things invented by the employee on the job with the employer's tools.

Specific provisions may be included relating to inventions and patents and to trade secrets. The employee may agree to assign to the employer all inventions, designs, and fabrications relating to the employer's business, and to assist in obtaining patents. A provision should also have the employee agree not to disclose any of the employer's trade secrets during or upon termination of employment. Such a clause generally covers known or used formulae, methods of production or sale, and customer lists.

SAMPLE

CONFIDENTIALITY (NON-DISCLOSURE) AGREEMENT

This NON-DISCLOSURE AGREEMENT ("Agreement") is made and entered into this ____ day of _____, 198_, by and between _____, Incorporated ("ABC"), a California corporation and _____, Inc., a California corporation (the "Company") (sometimes collectively referred to as the "Parties").

RECITALS

A. ABC is engaged in the business of _____ and has entered into discussion with the Company relating to a business relationship in connection with which ABC desires access to certain information relating to the Company.

B. The Company desires to maintain the confidentiality of the proprietary information disclosed to ABC, ABC is willing to receive all such proprietary information in confidence, and the Parties deem it to be in their best interest to protect such proprietary information in the form of this Agreement.

Now, therefore, in consideration of the mutual promises, agreements, covenants, conditions and undertakings herein contained, and for other good and valuable consideration, the receipt and sufficiency of which are hereby acknowledged, the parties agree as follows:

1.   Confidential Information.

1.1 To the extent that the Company shall disclose to ABC proprietary information concerning the Company's financial condition, business plan, products, manufacturing processes, inventions, patents, patent applications, secret processes, methods of operation and other proprietary information ("Confidential Information"), then all such Confidential Information disclosed to ABC shall be received by it in confidence for purposes of this Agreement unless otherwise exempted under the provisions of Section 5 hereof.

1.2 ABC, its directors, employees, agents and representatives shall not disclose, disseminate, publish, communicate or divulge any Confidential Information to anyone outside ABC, or to any employee of ABC not having access to such information, unless the Company expressly consents to such disclosure in writing.

2.   Term of Agreement.

This Agreement shall continue in full force and effect, both, during the period of any discussions between the Parties, and, if applicable, during the term of any subsequent agreement entered into between the Parties.

3.   Representations and Warranties.

3.1 The Company and ABC represent and warrant that their discussions do not and will not breach any agreement which either of them have to any other party to keep such information confidential.

3.2 ABC acknowledges that any failure by ABC to fulfill any obligation under this Agreement, or a breach by ABC of any provision herein, will constitute immediate and irreparable harm to the Company, which harm cannot be fully and adequately compensated in money damages and which will warrant injunctive relief, an order for specific performance, or other equitable relief.

4.   Liability.

ABC shall not be liable, under Section 1, for any of the following actions:

4.1 Disclosure of any information actually known to ABC prior to its receipt of Confidential Information under this Agreement, or information actually obtained from a source other than the Company.

4.2 Inadvertent disclosure of such Confidential Information where ABC has exercised reasonable care consistent with the effort ABC exercises with respect to the preservation of ABC's own confidential information.

4.3 Disclosure of such Confidential Information made with the prior written consent of the Company, as set forth in Section 1.2 herein.

4.4 Disclosure of such Confidential Information to others which necessarily results from the use of such information in connection with ABC's business.

5.   Return of Material.

Upon termination or expiration of this Agreement, ABC shall, upon the written request of Company, deliver any records, data, information and other documents and all copies thereof, furnished by the Company to ABC.

6.   General Provisions.

6.1 This Agreement supersedes any prior or contemporaneous agreement concerning the rights of the Parties with respect to Confidential Information.

6.2 This Agreement shall inure to the benefit of the Company, its successors, assigns and designees, and is binding upon the assigns, executors, administrators and other legal representatives of ABC.

6.3 This Agreement shall be construed in accordance with and governed for all purposes by the laws of the State of California. In case any one or more of the provisions contained in this Agreement shall, for any reason, be held to be invalid, illegal or unenforceable in any respect, such invalidity, illegality or unenforceability shall not affect any other provision of this Agreement, but this Agreement shall be construed as if such invalid, illegal or unenforceable provision had never been contained herein.

6.4 Any and all amendments, changes, revisions and discharges of this Agreement, in whole or in part, and from time to time, shall be binding upon the Parties so long as they are in writing and executed by the Parties hereto.

6.5 The failure of either party to enforce at any time, or for any period of time, the provisions of this Agreement shall not be construed as a waiver of such provision or of the right of such party thereafter to enforce each and every such provision.

6.6 In the event a dispute arises with respect to this Agreement, the party prevailing in such dispute shall be entitled to recover all expenses including, without limitation, reasonable attorneys' fees and expenses incurred in ascertaining such party's rights under this Agreement, whether or not it was necessary for such party to institute suit.

6.7 This Agreement and the rights and obligations of each of the Parties hereunder are personal to such Parties and may not, except as provided herein, be transferred or assigned, voluntarily or involuntarily, without the prior written consent of the other party.

6.8 This Agreement may be executed in several counterparts and when so executed shall constitute one agreement binding on all Parties, notwithstanding that all the Parties are not signatory to the original and same counterpart.

6.9 From time to time each party will execute and deliver such further instruments and will take such other action as any other party may reasonably request in order to discharge and perform their obligations and agreements hereunder and to give effect to the intentions expressed in this Agreement.

6.10 All exhibits referred to in this Agreement are incorporated herein in their entirety by such reference.

6.11 All cross-references in this Agreement, unless specifically directed to another agreement or document, refer to provisions in this Agreement, and shall not be deemed to be references to the overall transaction or to any other agreements or documents.

6.12 The various headings and numbers herein and the grouping of provisions of this Agreement into separate articles and paragraphs are for the purpose of convenience only and shall not be considered a part hereof. The language in all parts of this Agreement shall in all cases be construed in accordance with its fair meaning and not strictly for or against any one of the Parties.

IN WITNESS WHEREOF, the Parties have signed this Agreement as of the date set forth above.

ABC, INCORPORATED

By:_____
      President

THE COMPANY

By:_____
      President

SAMPLE

EMPLOYMENT AGREEMENT FOR EXECUTIVE

This Employment Agreement (the "Agreement") is entered into this ___ day of _____, 198_ ("Effective Date"), by and between _____, Inc., a California corporation ("Employer" or "the Company"), and _____, an individual ("Employee"), (both of whom are sometimes hereinafter referred to collectively as the "Parties" and each individually as a "Party").

RECITALS

A. Employer is in the business of _____.

B. Subject to the terms and conditions of this Agreement, Employer desires to employ Employee and Employee desires to be employed by Employer as Employer's _____ for a period of _____ years.

C. Both Employee and Employer desire to embody the terms and conditions of Employee's employment in a written agreement which will supersede all prior agreements of employment, whether written or oral.

Now, therefore, in consideration of the mutual covenants, duties, obligations and conditions contained herein, the parties agree as follows:

ARTICLE I

TERM OF EMPLOYMENT

Employer hereby employs Employee and Employee hereby accepts employment with Employer for a period of ___ years ("Term") commencing on the Effective Date, and terminating _____, 19__, unless sooner terminated as hereinafter provided.

ARTICLE II

DUTIES OF EMPLOYEE

2.1 <u>General</u>. Employee shall be employed in such executive capacities as Employer may determine from time to time, with the duties and powers customarily associated with such position, and shall perform such other duties pertaining to Employer's business as Employer may from time to time direct. Employee hereby consents to serve as an officer and director of Employer or any subsidiary or affiliate thereof without any additional salary or compensation. The base of operations of Employee shall be the principal office of Employer, or any other office of Employer within the State of California, unless changed by Employer, with the consent of Employee. If Employee shall render services to Employer at places other than the principal office of Employer, Employer agrees to either furnish such transportation and living expenses as may be reasonably required for Employee during and on account of the rendition of such services, or pay Employee a fixed weekly sum as reimbursement for such expenses incurred by Employee. In the latter regard, Employee agrees to keep records of such expenses and furnish Employer reasonably detailed reports of actual expenses incurred by Employee.

2.2 <u>Performance of Duties</u>. Employee agrees to devote his full time and efforts to the business and affairs of Employer, to use his best efforts to promote the interests of Employer and to faithfully, industriously and to the best of his ability, experience and talents, perform to the reasonable satisfaction of Employer all of the duties that may be assigned to him hereunder.

ARTICLE III

COMPENSATION AND OTHER EMPLOYEE BENEFITS

3.1 <u>Salary</u>. As compensation for his services rendered pursuant to this Agreement, Employer shall pay to Employee a salary, exclusive of bonus compensation, of $_____ per month, commencing with the Effective Date, payable in equal semimonthly installments during the Term hereof.

3.2 <u>Bonus</u>. <u>Salary Evaluation</u>. Evaluation of Employee's salary, as set forth in Section 3.1 hereof, shall occur at least once annually on each anniversary of the Effective Date during the Term of this Agreement.

3.3 <u>Automobile Expenses</u>. Employer shall reimburse Employee in the amount of $___ per mile for all out-of-pocket automobile expenses, subject to such written guidelines and/or requirements for verification as Employer may in its sole and absolute discretion require. Such expenses shall be accounted for by Employee and reimbursed by Employer on a monthly basis.

3.4 <u>Relocation; Moving Expenses</u>. The Parties acknowledge that Employee is required to change his place of residence from _____, _____ to _____, California to perform his duties under the terms of this Agreement. The Company shall pay or reimburse all the costs and expenses of Employee and his family connected with such relocation, including reasonable moving and travel expenses.

ARTICLE IV

DISCLOSURE OF INFORMATION

4.1 <u>Confidential Information</u>. Employee shall keep in strictest confidence all information relating to the business affairs, and customers of Employer, including, among other things, Employer's costs of performing services, pricing formulas, and/or methods of procedures, which Employee may acquire during the performance of his services and duties hereunder. Furthermore, during the Term of this Agreement, and at all times thereafter, Employee shall not publish, communicate, divulge, disclose or use, whether or not for his own benefit, any such information without the prior written consent of Employer.

Employee recognizes and acknowledges that Employer's trade secrets and proprietary information and processes, as they may exist from time to time, are valuable, special and unique assets of Employer's business, access to and knowledge of which are essential to the performance of the Employee's duties hereunder. Employee agrees that he/she will not, during or after the Term of his employment, in whole or in part, disclose such secrets, information or processes to any person, firm, corporation, association, or other entity for any reason or purpose whatsoever, nor shall Employee make use of any such property for his or her own purposes or for the benefit of any person, firm, corporation or other entity (except Employer) under any circumstances during or after the Term of his employment, provided that after the Term of his employment these restrictions shall not apply to such secrets, information and processes entering the public domain (provided that Employee was not responsible, directly or indirectly, for such secrets, information or processes entering the public domain) without Employer's consent. Employee agrees to hold as belonging to Employer, all property, memoranda, books, papers, letters, formulas and other data, and other copies thereof and therefrom, which in any way relate to Employer's business and affairs, whether made by him or otherwise coming into his possession, and on termination of his employment, or on demand of Employer, at any time, to deliver the same to Employer.

4.2 <u>Customer Information</u>. Employee hereby acknowledges that the identity of the customers of Employer and information which Employer has acquired or may acquire concerning those customers, whether or not the same originated through Employee's efforts, by virtue of the peculiar nature of Employer's business, are the sole property of Employer and constitute valuable trade secrets. Employee further agrees that he will not, either directly or indirectly, make known or divulge to any person, firm or corporation the names or addresses of any of the customers of Employer, whether such persons are customers of Employer as of the date hereof or become such in the future and whether or not such persons may become customers of Employer through the efforts of Employee and whether or not such persons have previously been customers of Employer. Employee further agrees that he will not, directly or indirectly, either for himself or for any other person, firm or corporation, call upon, solicit, divert or take away said customers of Employer at any time.

4.3 <u>Solicitation of Employees</u>. Employee acknowledges that important factors in Employer's business and operations are the loyalty and goodwill of its employees and its customers. Accordingly,

Employee agrees that after the expiration or termination of this Agreement he will not enter into, and will not participate in, any plan or arrangement to cause any of Employer's employees to terminate their employment with Employer or hire any of such employees for a period of two years in connection with any business initiated by Employee or any other person, firm or corporation.

     4.4 <u>Inventions</u>. Employee hereby sells, transfers and assigns to the Company or to any person, or entity designated by the Company, all of his or her entire right, title and interest in and to all inventions, ideas, disclosures and improvements, whether patented or unpatented, and copyrightable material, made or conceived by Employee, solely or jointly, in whole or in part, during or before the term hereof which (i) relate to methods, apparatus, designs, products, processes or devices sold, leased, used or under construction or development by the Company or any subsidiary; or (ii) otherwise relate or pertain to the business, functions or operations of the Company or any subsidiary; or (iii) arise (wholly or partly) from the efforts of Employee during the Term hereof. Employee shall communicate promptly and disclose to the Company, in such form as Employer request, all information, details and data pertaining to the aforementioned inventions, ideas, disclosures and improvements; and, whether during the Term hereof or thereafter, Employee shall execute and deliver to Company such formal transfers and assignments and such other papers and documents as may be required of Employee to permit Company or any person or entity designated by Employer to file and prosecute the patent applications and, as to copyrightable material, to obtain copyrights thereon.

     4.5 <u>Ongoing Obligation</u>. The provisions in this Article 4 shall be binding during Employee's employment and at all times thereafter, regardless of the circumstances or reasons for termination of this Agreement.

ARTICLE V

COVENANT NOT TO COMPETE

5.1 During the Term of this Agreement and, unless this Agreement is terminated pursuant to Article 6 hereof, for a period of 2 (two) years thereafter in the Counties of _____ in the State of California, Employee shall not compete, directly or indirectly, with Employer, interfere with, disrupt or attempt to disrupt the relationship, contractual or otherwise, between Employer and any customer, client, supplier, consultant or other employee of Employer. An activity competitive with an activity engaged in by Employer shall include, but not be limited to, becoming an employee, officer, consultant or director of, or being an investor in, or owner of, an entity or person engaged in substantially the business as then engaged in by Employer.

5.2 It is the desire and intent of the Parties that the provisions of this Section 5 shall be enforced to the fullest extent permissible under the laws and public policies applied in each jurisdiction in which enforcement is sought. Accordingly, if any particular portion of this Article 5 shall be adjudicated to be invalid or unenforceable, this Article 5 shall be deemed amended to delete therefrom the portion thus adjudicated to be invalid or unenforceable, such deletion to apply only with respect to the operation of this Section in the particular jurisdiction in which such adjudication is made.

ARTICLE VI

TERMINATION

This Agreement shall terminate:

(a)   Upon the death or permanent disability of Employee, "permanent disability" being defined as any continuous loss of one-half (1/2) or more of the time spent by Employee in the usual daily performance of his duties as a result of physical or mental illness for a continuous period of time deemed reasonable by the Board of Directors in its sole discretion.

(b)   At such time, if any, as Employer ceases to conduct business for any reason whatsoever.

(c)   At such time, if any, as Employee fails to comply with any applicable laws or regulation.

(d)   At the election of Employer, upon the breach by Employee of any term or condition of this Agreement, or upon the dismissal of Employee by Employer with or without cause.

ARTICLE VII

INSURANCE TAKEN BY EMPLOYER

Employer has the right to take insurance with respect to the performance of Employee's duties hereunder. If Employer should desire to obtain any form of insurance on or with respect to Employee, Employee agrees to cooperate with Employer in obtaining such insurance and agrees to submit to the usual and customary medical and other examinations requisite therefor, which said insurance shall be obtained at Employer's expense and for Employer's sole benefit during the term hereof.

ARTICLE VIII

REMEDY FOR BREACH

Employee acknowledges that the services to be rendered by him hereunder are of a special, unique and extraordinary character, which gives this Agreement a peculiar value to Employer, the loss of which cannot be reasonably or adequately compensated in damages in an action at law, and a breach by Employee of the provisions of this Agreement will cause Employer irreparable injury. It is, therefore, expressly acknowledged that this Agreement may be enforced by injunction and other equitable remedies, without bond. Such relief shall not be exclusive, but shall be in addition to any other rights or remedies Employer may have for such breach, and Employer shall be entitled to recover all costs and expense, including reasonable attorneys' fees, incurred by reason of any breach of the covenants of this Agreement.

ARTICLE IX

INDEMNIFICATION OF EMPLOYEE BY EMPLOYER

As a material consideration for Employee's entering into this Agreement, Employer shall indemnify and hold Employee harmless from and against any and all liabilities, losses, damages, costs and expenses, including but not limited to, court costs and reasonable attorneys' fees, which Employee may incur as a result of any contention, claim or cause of action brought against Employee seeking damages or injunctive relief as a result of any act of Employee performed in the course of his employment hereunder duly authorized by Employer. Employer covenants that it will reimburse Employee for, or pay over to Employee, all sums of money which Employee shall pay or become liable to pay by reason of any of the foregoing. If any suit, action or other proceeding is brought by any person against Employee pertaining in any way to any of the foregoing liabilities, Employer shall have the right, at its own expense, to control and direct the defense of any such suit, action or proceeding, and select counsel therefor. Employee shall have the right to adjust, settle or compromise any claim, suit or judgment against Employee pertaining to any of the foregoing liabilities.

ARTICLE X

MISCELLANEOUS

10.1   Notices.

All notices and other communications provided for or permitted hereunder shall be made by hand-delivery, first-class mail, telex or telecopier, addressed as follows:

If to Employer: _____
                     _____
                     _____

With a copy to: _____
                     _____
                     _____

If to Employee: _____
                     _____
                     _____

All such notices and communications given shall be deemed to have been duly given: when delivered by hand, if personally delivered; three (3) business days after deposit in any Untied States Post Office in the Continental United States, postage prepaid, if mailed; when answered back, if telexcd; and when receipt is acknowledged, if telecopied.

10.2   Attorneys' Fees.

In the event a dispute arises with respect to this Agreement, the party prevailing in such dispute shall be entitled to recover all expenses, including, without limitation, reasonable attorneys' fees and expenses, incurred in ascertaining such party's rights, in preparing to enforce, or in enforcing such party's rights under this Agreement, whether or not it was necessary for such party to institute suit.

10.3   Assignment.

This Agreement shall be binding upon and inure to the benefit of the parties hereto and the successors and assigns of Employer; provided, however, it is understood and agreed that the services to be rendered and the duties to be performed by Employee hereunder are of a special, unique and personal nature and that it would be difficult or impossible to replace such services; by reason thereof, Employee may not assign either the benefits or the obligations of this Agreement. Employee further agrees and consents that if he violates any of the provisions of this Agreement, the Employer, in addition to any other rights and remedies available under this Agreement or otherwise, shall be entitled to an injunction to be issued by a tribunal of competent jurisdiction, restraining the Employee from committing or continuing any violation of this Agreement.

10.4   <u>Extent of Agreement</u>.

The Employee certifies to Employer that he has read the foregoing Employment Agreement, that he fully understands its terms and conditions, that he has been assisted by independent counsel in understanding the terms of this Agreement, that the foregoing terms and conditions constitute his entire agreement with the Employer, and that no promise or understandings have been made other than those stated above.

10.5   <u>Employee Warranties</u>.

The Employee represents and warrants that his execution and performance of this Agreement does not and will not conflict with any other agreement to which he is a party or by which he is bound and will not violate any fiduciary obligation to any past or present employer.

10.6   <u>General Relationship</u>.

Employee shall be considered an employee of Employer within the meaning of all federal, state and local laws and regulations including, but not limited to, laws and regulations governing unemployment insurance, workmen's compensation, industrial accident, labor and taxes.

10.7   <u>Hiring At Will</u>.

The continuance of Employee's employment by Employer after the Term of this Agreement shall be deemed a hiring at will and shall be subject to termination with or without cause by either Employer or Employee upon delivery of notice thereof to the other party. Except with respect to the foregoing termination provisions, any such continuance of employment shall be upon the same terms and conditions as are set forth herein.

10.8   Complete Agreement of the Parties.

This Agreement supersedes any and all other agreements, either oral or in writing, between the parties with respect to the subject matter hereof and contains all of the covenants and agreements between the parties with respect to such subject matter in any manner whatsoever. Each party to this Agreement acknowledges that no representations, inducements, promises or agreements, oral or otherwise, have been made by any party, or anyone herein, and that no other agreement, statement or promise not contained in this Agreement shall be valid or binding. This Agreement may be changed or amended only by an amendment in writing signed by all of the parties or their respective successors-in-interest.

10.9   Binding.

This Agreement shall be binding upon and inure to the benefit of the successors-in-interest, assigns and personal representatives of the respective parties.

10.10   Number and Gender.

Whenever a singular number is used in this Agreement and when required by the context, the same shall include the plural, and the masculine gender shall include the feminine and neuter genders and the word "person" shall include corporate, firm, partnership or other form of association.

10.11   Failure to Object Not a Waiver.

The failure of either party to this Agreement to object to, or to take affirmative action with respect to, any conduct of the other which is in violation of the terms of this Agreement, shall not be construed as a waiver of the violation or breach or of any future violation, breach or wrongful conduct.

10.12 Unenforceable Terms.

Any provision hereof prohibited by law or unenforceable under any applicable law of any jurisdiction shall as to such jurisdiction be ineffective without affecting any other provision of this Agreement. To the full extent, however, that the provisions of such applicable law may be waived, they are hereby waived to the end that this Agreement be deemed to be a valid and binding agreement enforceable in accordance with its terms.

10.13 Execution in Counterparts.

This Agreement may be executed in several counterparts and when so executed shall constitute one agreement binding on all the parties, notwithstanding that all the parties are not signatory to the original and same counterpart.

10.14 Further Assurance.

From time to time each party will execute and deliver such further instruments and will take such other action as any other party may reasonably request in order to discharge and perform their obligations and agreements hereunder and to give effect to the intentions expressed in this Agreement.

10.15 Incorporation By Reference.

All exhibits referred to in this Agreement are incorporated herein in their entirety by such reference.

10.16 Cross-References.

All cross-references in this Agreement, unless specifically directed to another agreement or document, refer to provisions in this Agreement, and shall not be deemed to be references to the overall transactions or to any other agreements or documents.

10.17   Miscellaneous Provisions.

The various headings and numbers herein and the grouping of provisions of this Agreement into separate articles and paragraphs are for the purpose of convenience only and shall not be considered a part hereof. The language in all parts of this Agreement shall in all cases be construed to its fair meaning as if prepared by all parties to the Agreement and not strictly for or against any of the parties.

IN WITNESS WHEREOF, the parties hereto have executed this Agreement on the day and year first hereinabove set forth.

EMPLOYER: EMPLOYEE:

By:_____   _____
Title:_____

CONSULTING AGREEMENT

In certain situations an alternative to an employment agreement may be a consulting agreement. A consulting agreement usually involves an independent contractor relationship which prohibits the corporation from exercising too much control over the consultant. The consulting agreement is normally used if the relationship will be for a particular project or purpose.

An employer contemplating a consulting agreement should consider a number of facts. To begin, an employer should determine how long the project will take to be completed. If the project will be ongoing or require regular maintenance, an employment contract may be preferable. Next, the employer should consider how much control he or she wishes to exercise over the project. Whether a consulting agreement or employment agreement is drafted, an employer should determine how much control he or she will want to exercise over the design, material to be used, and actual production. Finally, it is a good idea to find out if the type of services needed are generally rendered on a consulting agreement or employment agreement basis. Once this is determined, specific provisions can be added to limit or authorize certain business activity.

The sample consulting agreement, which follows, contains many of the same general provisions found in an employment agreement. Terms relating to employee compensations and remedy for breach should be drafted with special care. The terms should be as specific as possible and attempt to anticipate concerns which are inherent to the particular business.

SAMPLE

CONSULTING AGREEMENT

This Consulting Agreement ("Agreement") is entered into effective as of _____, 198_, by and between _____, Inc., a California corporation ("Company"), and _____, an individual ("Consultant").

RECITALS

Company wishes to obtain the consulting services of Consultant to assist Company in connection with _____, and Consultant is willing to provide such services, on the terms and conditions set forth herein.

AGREEMENT

NOW, THEREFORE, in consideration of the mutual agreements and promises contained herein, the parties hereby agree as follows:

1. Term of Agreement

Company hereby engages Consultant and Consultant accepts such engagement for a term of _____ years commencing _____, 198_, and terminating _____, 19__, unless sooner terminated as hereinafter provided.

2. Services of Consultant

Consultant agrees to provide to Company, as requested by Company, the following advice and consulting services:

[INSERT SERVICES]

Consultant shall provide such advice and services through an officer or employee of Consultant that is acceptable to Company. The term "Consulting Agent" may be used herein to refer to such officer or employee of Consultant.

3. Necessary Services

3.1 <u>Performance of Duties</u>. Consultant agrees that he shall cause the Consulting Agent to at all times faithfully, industriously, and to the best of his ability, experience, and talents perform all of the duties that may reasonably be assigned to him hereunder and, subject to the provisions of subsection 3.2, devote such time to the performance of such duties as may be necessary therefor.

3.2 <u>Part-time Service</u>. During the term of this Agreement the Consulting Agent shall be available on a part-time basis to perform the duties assigned to him hereunder. "Part-time basis" is hereby defined as _____ hours per week for _____ weeks per year.

4. Compensation

In consideration for the services required of Consultant hereunder, Company agrees to compensate Consultant as follows:

4.1 <u>Retainer</u>. Company shall pay to Consultant the sum of _____ Dollars. Such sum shall be payable in accordance with written instructions to be delivered to Company by Consultant.

4.2 <u>Stock</u>. Company shall deliver to Consultant _____ shares of the Common Stock of _____ Corporation, a California corporation. All such shares shall be restricted with respect to resale pursuant to Rule 144 promulgated by the Securities and Exchange Commission pursuant to the Securities Act of 1933, as amended, and Company shall deliver such shares to Consultant at such times and in such one or more portions as Consultant shall specify by written notice to Company. Each such delivery shall be made within ten (10) days after Company's receipt of Consultant's written notice requesting such delivery.

       4.3<u>Expense Reimbursement</u> Company shall reimburse Consultant for any out-of-pocket expenses incurred in connection with the negotiation and execution of this Agreement and the performance of services required of Consultant hereunder.

5. <u>Independent Contractor</u>

       In performing services and duties hereunder, Consultant and any person acting on Consultant's behalf shall do so as independent contractors and are not, and are not to be deemed, employees or agents of Company or any other person acting on behalf of Company. Consultant shall be responsible for meeting any legal requirements imposed on Consultant or any person acting on his behalf as a result of this Agreement, including but not limited to the filing of income tax returns and the payment of taxes; and Consultant agrees to indemnify Company for the failure to do so, if Company is required to make any such payment otherwise due by Consultant or any such person acting on Consultant's behalf.

6. <u>Remedy for Breach</u>

       Consultant acknowledges that the services to be rendered by him hereunder are of a special, unique, and extraordinary character which gives this Agreement a peculiar value to Company, the loss of which cannot be reasonably or adequately compensated in damages in an action at law, and that a breach by Consultant of this Agreement shall cause Company irreparable injury. Therefore, Consultant expressly acknowledges that this Agreement may be enforced against him by injunction and other equitable remedies, without bond. Such relief shall not be exclusive, but shall be in addition to any other rights or remedies Company may have for such breach.

7. Termination

    7.1 Causes for Termination. This Agreement shall terminate immediately upon the occurrence of any one of the following events:

        7.1.1   The expiration of the term hereof;

        7.1.2   The written agreement of the parties;

        7.1.3   The occurrence of circumstances that make it impossible for the business of Company to be continued;

        7.1.4   Consultant's breach of his duties hereunder, unless waived by Company or cured by Consultant within 30 days after Company's having given written notice thereof to Consultant; and

        7.1.5   Company's breach of his duties to Consultant hereunder, unless waived by Consultant or cured by Company within 30 days after Consultant's having given written notice thereof to Company.

    7.2 Compensation upon Termination. Unless otherwise mutually agreed in writing by the parties, the termination of this Agreement due to any cause other than that specified in subsection

7.1.4 shall not relieve Company of his obligation to make any payment of money or any delivery of shares or securities which would have been required, or could have been required by Consultant, pursuant to Sections 4.1, 4.2 and 4.3, if this Agreement had not been so terminated.

8.   General Provisions

8.1<u>Survival of Agreement</u>. This Agreement and the rights and obligations of the parties hereto shall not be terminated by reason of (i) the merger, reorganization, or consolidation of Company, (ii) the transfer of all or substantially all of the assets of Company, or (iii) the voluntary or involuntary dissolution of Company. In the event of any such merger, reorganization, consolidation or transfer of assets, the surviving or resulting corporation or transferee of such assets shall be bound by and shall have the benefit of the provisions of this Agreement, and Company shall take all actions necessary to insure that such corporation or transferee is bound by the provisions of this Agreement.

8.2<u>Legal Representation</u>.   Each of the parties expressly acknowledges and agrees that he has consulted with and utilized separate counsel in connection with this Agreement.

8.3<u>Notices</u>. All notices and other communications provided for or permitted hereunder shall be in writing and shall be made by hand delivery, first class mail, telex or telecopier, addressed as follows:

<u>PARTY</u>   <u>ADDRESS</u>

All such notices and communications shall be deemed to have been duly given when delivered by hand, if personally delivered; three (3) business days after deposit in any United States Post Office in the Continental United States, postage prepaid, if mailed; when answered back, if telexed; and when receipt is acknowledged, if telecopied.

8.4<u>Attorneys' Fees</u>. I n the event that a dispute arises with respect to this Agreement, the party prevailing in such dispute shall be entitled to recover all expenses, including, without limitation, reasonable attorneys' fees and expenses, incurred in ascertaining such party's rights or in preparing to enforce, or in enforcing, such party's rights under this Agreement, whether or not it was necessary for such party to institute suit.

8.5<u>Complete Agreement of the Parties</u>. This Agreement supersedes any and all other agreements, either oral or in writing, between the parties with respect to the subject matter hereof and contains all of the covenants and agreements between the parties with respect to such subject matter in any manner whatsoever. Each party acknowledges that no representations, inducements, promises or agreements, oral or otherwise, have been made by any other party, or anyone herein, and that no other agreement, statement, or promise not contained in this Agreement shall be valid or binding. This Agreement may be changed or amended only by an amendment in writing signed by all of the parties or their respective successors in interest.

8.6<u>Assignment</u>. This Agreement shall be binding upon and inure to the benefit of the parties and the successors and assigns of Company; provided however, it is understood and agreed that the services to be rendered and the duties to be performed by Consultant through its agent as specified hereunder are of a special, unique, and personal nature and that it would be difficult or impossible to replace such services; by reason thereof, Consultant may not assign either the benefits or the obligations of this Agreement. Consultant further agrees and consents that if it violates any of the provisions of this Agreement, Company, in addition to any other rights or remedies available under this Agreement or otherwise, shall be entitled to an injunction to be issued by a tribunal of competent jurisdiction, restraining Consultant from committing or continuing any violation of this Agreement.

8.7<u>Binding</u>. This Agreement shall be binding upon and inure to the benefit of the successors in interest, assigns, and personal representatives of the respective parties.

8.8<u>Number and Gender</u>. Whenever the singular number is used in this Agreement and when required by the context, the same shall include the plural. The masculine gender shall include the feminine and neuter genders, and the word "person" shall include a corporation, firm, partnership, or other form of association.

8.9<u>Governing Law</u>. The parties hereby expressly acknowledge and agree that this Agreement is entered into in the State of California and, to the extent permitted by law, this Agreement shall be construed and enforced in accordance with the laws of the State of California.

8.10 <u>Failure to Object Not a Waiver</u>. The failure of a party to object to, or to take affirmative action with respect to, any conduct of the other which is in violation of the terms of this Agreement shall not be construed as a waiver of the violation or breach or of any future violation, breach, or wrongful conduct.

8.11 <u>Unenforceable Terms</u>. Any provision hereof prohibited or unenforceable under any applicable law of any jurisdiction shall as to such jurisdiction be ineffective without affecting any other provision of this Agreement. To the full extent, however, that the provisions of such applicable law may be waived, they are hereby waived to the end that this Agreement be deemed to be a valid and binding agreement enforceable in accordance with its terms.

8.12 <u>Execution In Counterparts</u>. This Agreement may be executed in several counterparts and when so executed shall constitute one agreement binding on all the parties, notwithstanding that all the parties are not signatory to the original and same counterpart.

8.13 <u>Further Assurance</u>. From time to time each party shall execute and deliver such further instruments and shall take such other action as any other party may reasonably request in order to discharge and perform their obligations and agreements hereunder and to give effect to the intentions expressed in this Agreement.

8.14 <u>Incorporation By Reference</u>. All exhibits referred to in this Agreement are incorporated herein in their entirety by such reference.

8.15 <u>Cross-References</u>. All cross-references in this Agreement, unless specifically directed to another agreement or document, refer to provisions in this Agreement, and shall not be deemed to be references to any overall transaction or to any other agreements or documents.

8.16 <u>Miscellaneous Provisions</u>. The various headings and numbers herein and the grouping of provisions of this Agreement into separate divisions are for the purpose of convenience only and shall not be considered a part hereof. The language in all parts of this Agreement shall in all cases be construed in accordance to its fair meaning as if prepared by all parties to the Agreement and not strictly for or against any of the parties.

IN WITNESS WHEREOF, the parties have executed this Agreement on the date first written above.

COMPANY: CONSULTANT:

_____   _____

_____
By:

FINANCING

Once a relationship is established with independent contractors and employees, certain financing may be needed which in most instances will require that the corporation sign a promissory note. More times than not, the president of a small, closely-held corporation which is just beginning its operations will be asked to sign personally and not in her or his capacity as president of the corporation.

The two forms of promissory notes set forth below are for a corporate signature. This is most beneficial since if the corporation defaults on its payments the creditor may only look to the corporation for collection and not to an individual who may have signed the promissory note personally - not in his capacity as president of the corporation.

The first promissory note is a demand promissory note which means that the funds are due upon demand. The second promissory note entitles the maker to pay off both the principal and interest over a specified period of time. The acknowledgement which follows the second promissory note may be used in conjunction with either note and is a representation that the officer signing on behalf of the corporation making the note is the person he/she alleges to be.

SAMPLE

PROMISSORY DEMAND NOTE

_____, California   _____, 198_

On demand, _____, Inc., (the "Borrower"), for value received, promises to pay to the order of _____, Inc., a California corporation ("Lender"), at the office of Lender at _____, California _____, the sum of $_____ and interest at an annual rate of _____percent (___%).

Payments of principal and interest are to be made in lawful money of the United States of America.

The Borrower further agrees, subject only to any limitation imposed by applicable law, to pay all expenses, including reasonable attorney's fees and legal expenses, incurred by the holder of this Note in endeavoring to collect any amounts payable hereunder which are not paid when due, whether by acceleration or otherwise.

All Parties to this Note hereby waive presentment and notice of demand, protest and notice of protest and non-payment of this Note.

IN WITNESS WHEREOF, this Promissory Demand Note has been executed by the undersigned as of the ____ day of 19__.

_____, Inc.

_____

By:_____, President

SAMPLE

PROMISSORY NOTE

$_____   _____, CA
Due:_____, 198_   Date:_____, 198_

      FOR VALUE RECEIVED, _____, Inc. (the "Maker"), promises to pay to the order of _____ or his assigns ("Payee"), the principal sum of _____ Dollars ($_____) together with interest at a rate equal to _____ percent (__%) per annum on the outstanding principal balance. Interest shall be paid in __ consecutive monthly installments, commencing on _____, 198_ and on the ___th day of each successive month.

      All payments made by Maker shall be applied first against the interest due for the applicable month and then against the unpaid principal balance. Both principal and interest shall be paid at the business address of Payee at _____, California or at such other place as the Payee shall have designated to the Maker in writing.

      This Note may be prepaid in whole and will not be subject to a prepayment penalty.

      The Maker hereby waives presentment, demand, protest and notice except as provided above. The Maker shall pay on demand all costs, including court costs and reasonable attorneys' fees, paid or incurred by Payee hereof in enforcing this Promissory Note upon the occurrence of any event of default.

Any notice or demand upon Maker shall be deemed to have been given or served for all purposes hereof when mailed, by registered or certified mail, postage prepaid at the business address of Maker, or at such other business address as Maker may designate in writing from time to time.

This Promissory Note is a contract made under the laws of the State of California and, together with the rights and obligations of Payee and Maker, shall be construed, interpreted and enforced under the laws of the State of California.

IN WITNESS WHEREOF, the Maker has caused this Promissory Note to be signed by its duly authorized officer, as of the date first above written.

By:_____, President

SAMPLE

ACKNOWLEDGMENT

STATE OF_____)

COUNTY OF_____)

     Before me, the undersigned authority, on this day personally appeared _____, known to me to be the officer whose name is subscribed to the foregoing instrument, and acknowledged to me that the same was the act of _____, Inc., a California corporation, and that he executed the same as the act of such corporation for the purposes and consideration therein expressed and in the capacity therein stated.

     Given under my hand and seal of office, this __ day of _____, 198_.

_____
NOTARY PUBLIC

BUSINESS AGREEMENTS

Certain documents and agreements are customary in the daily operations of most business entities. These agreements range from basic to sophisticated and are appropriate for certain specific business needs. Many companies which manufacture or develop products are in need of a contract for the sale of goods. This type of contract may have a variety of provisions relating to the payment of the purchase price and the method of delivery. In addition, the obligation to purchase the product in installments may be incorporated into the terms of the agreement. The following sample is intended as a model only in circumstances which require protection for the seller.

Please note that with respect to contracts in the ordinary course of the company's business, middle management officer/employees may be given authority by the board of directors to enter into contracts on behalf of the company. Other commitments may be reserved to other board committees, or even withheld by the board of directors from committees.

Some transactions may be of such magnitude, or so far from the usual course of business, that even senior management or the board of directors would not have full authority to conclude it. For example, a sale of substantially all a company's assets would require shareholder approval. A long-term lease, a sale or purchase of real estate, or any major acquisition might require board approval, or at least some evidence of board-delegated authority. When preparing the documents for such a transaction, care should be taken that the signing officer has sufficient authority, either in the Bylaws or in board resolutions to enter into the transaction and sign the agreement on behalf of the corporation.

California law states that in the absence of actual knowledge of lack of authority, a person entering into a contract with a corporation may rely on that contract if it is signed by the chairman of the board; the president; or a vice-president and the secretary, an assistant secretary, the chief financial officer, or an assistant treasurer. However, in order to give assurance that the person signing on behalf of the corporation has the proper authority, an "incumbency certificate" to that effect may be required. An incumbency certificate is a certificate that assures that a person is duly appointed and qualified to make a contract binding on the corporation; the certificate is furnished by the secretary of the corporation and usually bears the corporate seal attesting to the secretary's incumbency. Sometimes a further certificate as to the secretary's incumbency is required. The certificate should set forth the signatures of the designated officers in order to prevent the possibility of their misuse by others.

SAMPLE

CERTIFICATE OF INCMUBENCY

I hereby certify that the following is a true and correct copy of the resolution adopted by unanimous written consent (or at a meeting duly called and held) of the Board of Directors of _____, Inc., a California corporation, on _____, 19__, that it has not been changed and remains in full force and effect:

[SET FORTH RESOLUTIONS]

IN WITNESS WHEREOF, the undersigned has executed this Certificate on _____, 19__.

_____
_____, Secretary

SAMPLE

CONTRACT FOR THE SALE OF GOODS

This contract for the sale of goods ("Agreement") is made and entered into this _____ day of _____, 198_ by and between ABC Corporation ("ABC") and _____ (the "Company") (sometimes collectively referred to as the "Parties" or individually as a "Party").

<u>RECITALS</u>

A. ABC is engaged in the business of _____.

B. ABC has copyrighted _____ (the "Product").

C. ABC desires to sell to the Company and the Company desires to buy from ABC the Product in accordance with the terms of this Agreement.

Now, therefore, in consideration of the mutual promises, agreements, covenants, conditions and undertakings herein contained, and for other good and valuable consideration, the receipt and sufficiency of which are hereby acknowledged, the parties agree as follows:

1. <u>Sale</u>. The Parties agree that the Company will purchase, on the date of execution of this Agreement, _____ Products (the "Initial Order") pursuant to the terms of Sections 2 and 3 below. The Parties further agree that the Company will have fifteen (15) days from the date of execution of this Agreement to evaluate the Products and determine if it will commit to the purchase of an additional __ Products (the "Additional Purchases") subject to the terms of Section 4 below.

2. <u>Purchase Price</u>. The parties agree that the Company will purchase the Initial Order for a flat rate of $_____. Payment to be made in accordance with the provisions of Section 3. The Parties further agree that any Additional Purchases will be in accordance with the price schedule attached hereto as Exhibit "A" and incorporated herein by this reference.

3. <u>Terms of Payment</u>. Terms of payment are net cash upon delivery of the Initial Order and the Additional Purchases to the Company. ABC reserves the right to require payment in advance of delivery, upon written notification to the Company, if in ABC's sole opinion, the Company's financial condition or other circumstances so warrant.

4. <u>Additional Purchases</u>. If prior to the expiration of the fifteen (15) day period referenced in Section 1 above, the Company decides to purchase the Additional Products, it must so notify ABC in writing. Such Additional Purchases will be delivered in accordance with the terms of delivery set forth in Sections 6 and 7 below. In the event, the Company should decide, prior to the expiration of the fifteen (15) day period not to make the Additional Purchases it must so notify ABC in writing and this Agreement shall be considered completed and terminated by the Parties. In the event the Company fails to notify ABC of acceptance or rejection of the Additional Purchases, the Company expressly agrees that such failure to notify ABC shall be deemed an acceptance and ABC shall deliver the Additional Purchases in accordance with the terms of this Agreement and the Company shall be responsible for the payment of such Additional Purchases.

5. <u>Right of ABC to Increase Prices</u>. In the event that ABC finds, prior to delivery of the Products under this Agreement, that the cost of production for any reason whatsoever has become so great, as determined in the sole opinion of ABC, that it cannot deliver the

Products covered by this Agreement at the price herein stated, it shall have the right to increase such price upon giving ten (10) days written notice of such increase to the Company. In that event, the Company shall within three (3) days, from the date of ABC's notification, notify ABC in writing whether or not it will purchase the Products at the increased price. In the event that the Company fails to notify ABC within this three (3) day period, such failure to notify such expressly be construed by the Parties as an acceptance of the increased price. In the event that the Company notifies ABC that it refuses to pay such increased prices, then this Agreement shall at once terminate, and neither Party shall be liable to the other hereunder.

　　　6. <u>Delivery in Installments</u>. The Additional Purchases shall be delivered to the Company in installments of _____ Products per month for the next _____ months, on the fifteenth day of each month, the final installment to be delivered on the fifteenth of _____, 198_. Each delivery is to be made to the Company at _____, California, or as otherwise provided by the Company upon written notification to ABC within fifteen (15) days of the next delivery date. ABC agrees to deliver the Product to a carrier for transportation to the Company and to the carrier for transportation thereof to the address set forth above. The Company opts to bear all risk of loss from the time the goods are deposited with the carrier and transportation charges in connection with the delivery of the Product.

　　　7. <u>Installment Deliveries as Separate Sales</u>. It is understood and agreed by the Parties that the Company shall be liable to pay the agreed price for each installment without regard to the failure to deliver subsequent installments of such Products. Nor shall ABC's failure to deliver any installment give the Company the right to refuse to receive any other installment even though such failure to deliver substantially impairs the value of the entire Agreement.

8.   <u>Acceptance of Products</u>.   The Company agrees that acceptance and payment of the Products under this Agreement satisfies all of ABC's obligations and after acceptance the Company shall have no remedy against ABC whatsoever, nor may the Company revoke its acceptance for any reason whatsoever.

9.   <u>Protection of Copyright</u>. The Company acknowledges that the Products contain proprietary material originally developed by ABC and are protected by a copyright to ABC. The Company agrees that it will not do any act which it knows, or has reason to know, or is so notified by ABC, that may affect the validity of the content of the Products or the copyright (the "Proprietary Material"). The Company agrees that it will take all reasonable measures to preserve and protect the Proprietary Material and the rights of ABC thereto and to ensure that the customers of the Company are apprised of the proprietary nature of the Products and the copyright associated therewith. The Company further agrees that it will not reproduce or grant the right to reproduce the Products to any other party.

10.   <u>General Provisions</u>.

10.01 This Agreement supersedes any prior or contemporaneous agreement concerning the rights of the Parties under this Agreement.

10.02 Any and all amendments, changes, revisions and of this Agreement, in whole or in part, and from time to time, shall be binding upon the Parties so long as they are in writing and executed by the Parties hereto.

10.03 In the event a dispute arises with respect to this Agreement, the Party prevailing in such dispute shall be entitled to recover all expenses including, without limitation, reasonable attorneys' fees and expenses incurred in ascertaining such Party's rights under this Agreement, whether or not it was necessary for such Party to institute suit.

10.04 This Agreement and the rights and obligations of each of the Parties hereunder are personal to such Parties and may not, except with the prior written consent of the other Party, be transferred or assigned, voluntarily or involuntarily, without the prior written consent of the other Party.

10.05 This Agreement may be executed in several counterparts and when so executed shall constitute one agreement binding on the Parties, notwithstanding that all the Parties are not signatory to the original and same counterpart.

10.06 From time to time each Party will execute and deliver such further instruments and will take such other action as any other Party may reasonably request in order to discharge and perform their obligations and agreements hereunder and to give effect to the intentions expressed in this Agreement.

10.07 All exhibits referred to in this Agreement are incorporated herein in their entirety by such reference.

IN WITNESS WHEREOF, the Parties have signed this Agreement as of the date set forth above.

THE COMPANY

By:_____

ABC

By:_____

STOCK SALES

Various other types of sophisticated business agreements are necessary if the company is considering the sale of its assets or stock. There are many legal, tax, and accounting considerations in these types of transactions and it is essential that an attorney be involved in the negotiation and structuring of the transaction. As samples, the following asset purchase, stock purchase, buy-sell, and joint venture agreement provide information on the essential terms of these four different types of transactions.

The specific business points of an asset purchase or stock purchase must be adequately reflected in the agreements. These samples portray only generic points which are found in the standard sale or joint venture. It is important to note that the sale of stock constitutes the sale of a security, as does the sale of a limited partnership interest. An attorney must, therefore, carefully review federal and state securities laws for their applicability to the proposed transaction.

The sale of a corporation's stock is different from the sale of its assets. In a sale of assets, the corporation is the seller, but in a sale of stock the shareholders are the sellers. It is very important to understand this distinction, because each transaction carries different benefits and liabilities.

To begin, a purchase of a controlling share in a corporation ordinarily carries with it the debts and liabilities of the corporation, while a purchaser of assets generally does not assume the debts and obligations of the business. There are, however, exceptions in both cases. For instance, in a stock purchase agreement, the parties may specifically agree to waive certain liabilities. Similarly, in an asset purchase agreement there are certain debts and obligations that may be assumed by the buyer of the assets, even without an agreement to do so.

Next, the sale of stock requires qualification, or permission or clearance from the State Corporations Commissioner, a complication which can be avoided by selling the assets only. The sale of assets, however, involves requirements which do not have to be addressed in a sale of stock. For example, in a sale of assets, individual documents of transfer, such as deeds, and assignments and bills of sale must be prepared. Additionally, the sale of the personal property of the business may be subject to a sales tax.

Further, a business whose loans are secured by its assets require the lender's consent before the transfer of the assets can take place. Generally, the sale of stock does not require the lender's consent.

It is also important to understand the assumption of prior obligations in each of these transactions. In a sale of stock, the buyer ordinarily assumes the existing debts, taxes and other liabilities of the company if controlling stock is purchased. In an asset purchase agreement, the buyer does not generally assume these liabilities unless the parties specifically agree to them.

Finally, stock purchase and asset purchase agreements may have different voting requirements. For the sale of stock, a majority may be required, but the articles or bylaws may require the approval of a larger proportion of the shareholders. A sale of the assets of a corporation must be approved by at least a majority of the voting shares of the corporation.

The buy-sell agreement set forth below is used primarily in connection with a shareholders' agreement, which does not have this provision recited directly within the agreement (the shareholder's agreement included in this book does have buy-sell provisions) or in connection with the issuance of stock when the party issuing the stock desires to have a right of first refusal to re-purchase the stock if the party to who it is issued intends to dispose of it.

Please note that a transaction such as the sale of stock or sale of assets significantly alters the capital structure of the corporation and the existing rights of the shareholders and therefore requires shareholder approval. In California, the Secretary of the corporation may execute and deliver a certificate attached to an instrument transferring title which will attest that the transaction was validly approved by the board, and that either the property is less than substantially all the assets of the company, or that the transfer is in the usual and regular course of business. Alternatively, if the transaction is a sale of substantially all of the assets, and is not in the regular course of business, the certificate would reflect that fact, and also confirm that the required shareholders' approval was obtained. The certificate is prima facie ("on its face") evidence of the facts recited, and is conclusive as to any innocent purchaser or encumbrancer for value.

SAMPLE

BUY-SELL AGREEMENT

This Buy-Sell Agreement (the "Agreement") is made and entered into this ____ day of _____, 198__, by and among _____, a California corporation ("_____), and _____, ("_____") _____ ("_____") (hereinafter collectively referred to as the "Shareholders," which term shall include any transferee of any of the shares of _____, presently held by any of the above-listed individuals), and _____, a California corporation (hereinafter referred to as the "Corporation"), and is made with reference to the following facts:

A. Each of the Shareholders presently owns the following number of the Corporation's issued and outstanding shares of common stock (the "Shares"):

<u>Names</u>   <u>Shares</u>

B. In order to provide for the stability of the Corporation and to promote continuity of its management and policies, the Shareholders desire to restrict the manner and means by which the Shares may be sold, assigned or otherwise transferred.

NOW, THEREFORE, in consideration of the mutual benefits to be derived herefrom and of the mutual agreements hereinafter set forth, thee parties hereto agree as follows:

1.   RESTRICTION ON TRANSFER OF SHARES.

1.1<u>Restriction on Shares</u>. None of the Shares now or hereafter owned or held by any of the Shareholders or their successors and assigns, may be sold, assigned, transferred, pledged, hypothecated, granted, or in any other way disposed of or encumbered, voluntarily or involuntarily, by gift, testamentary disposition, inheritance, transfers to a voting or inter vivos trust, seizure and sale by legal process, operation of law, bankruptcy, winding up of a corporation, or otherwise, except in accordance with the terms of this Agreement. Furthermore, during such time, if any, as the corporation is an electing small business corporation under Subchapter S of the Internal Revenue Code of 1954, as amended, no Shares may be disposed of to an entity or person whose ownership of such Shares would render the Corporation ineligible to be taxed as an electing small business corporation. No sale, transfer or other disposition of Shares shall be valid, effective, entitled to recognition for any purpose, including voting or dividend rights, or made on the books of the Corporation if made in violation of the provisions of this Agreement.

2.   OPTIONAL PURCHASES.

2.1<u>Voluntary Sales, Transfers and Encumbrances</u>. In the event any Shareholder desires to encumber or dispose of all or any part of his Shares, or any interest therein, whether by sale, gift, pledge, hypothecation, transfer in trust, or otherwise, he shall serve written notice upon the Corporation of his intention to do so. The notice shall be accompanied by an executed counterpart of any document of transfer, which must name the proposed transferee and specify the number of Shares to be transferred, the price per Share, and the terms of payment. Promptly upon receipt of such notice, the secretary of the Corporation shall forward a copy of the notice and executed counterpart to every other Shareholder and to each member of the Corporation's board of directors, and within ten (10) days thereafter a meeting of the board of directors shall be duly called, noticed, and held to consider the proposed transfer.

For thirty (30) days following its receipt of such notice the Corporation shall have the option to purchase all or part of such Shares. If the proposed transfer is by sale, the option shall be at the price and on the terms stated in the notice. If the proposed transfer is by voluntary transfer other than by sale, the Corporation shall have the option to purchase all or part of such Shares at the price and on the terms and conditions specified in Paragraphs 5 and 6 of this Agreement. If the Corporation elects to exercise its option within the thirty (30) day period, the secretary of the Corporation shall give written notice of that fact to the offering Shareholder and the Corporation shall then purchase such Shares at the purchase price and upon the terms set forth in this Agreement or in the notice of intention to transfer, whichever is applicable.

If the option is not exercised by the Corporation as to all Shares set forth in the notice of intention to transfer within the thirty (30) day period, the Shareholder desiring to encumber or dispose of this Shares shall immediately serve notice of the proposed transfer in the same form as the notice given to the Corporation to the remaining Shareholders, who for a period of fifteen (15) days following their receipt of the notice shall have the option to purchase any Shares not purchased by the Corporation at the price and on the same terms and conditions as given to the Corporation. Any Shareholder desiring to acquire any part or all of the Shares offered shall deliver to the Shareholder desiring to encumber or dispose of his Shares a written notice of his election to purchase the Shares or a specified number of them. If the total number of Shares specified in the elections exceeds the number of available Shares, each Shareholder shall have priority, up to the number of shares specified in his notice of election, to purchase such proportion of the available Shares as the number of Shares owned by him bears to the total number of Shares owned by all Shareholders electing to purchase. Any Shares not purchased on such a priority basis shall be allocated in one or more successive allocations to those Shareholders electing to purchase more than the number of Shares as to which they have a priority right, up to the number of Shares specified in their respective notices, in the same proportion as the number of Shares owned by each of them bears to the number of Shares owned by all of the Shareholders electing to purchase Shares in excess of those as to which they have a priority right.

Notwithstanding the foregoing, the options extended to the Corporation and the other Shareholders may be exercised only if the Corporation and/or the other Shareholders elect to acquire all of the offered Shares.

If the Corporation and the other Shareholders do not purchase all of the Shares set forth in the notice of intention to transfer, the offered Shares may be transferred at any time within sixty (60) days after the date of the termination of the Shareholders' options upon the terms specified in the notice, except that no such sales or transfers shall be valid or effective for any purpose whatsoever, unless the purchaser(s), transferee(s), or encumbrancer(s) of such Shares shall agree (a) to continue the Corporation's status as an electing small business corporation, if such election is then in effect, (b) to be bound by the terms and conditions of this Agreement, and (c) in the case of a pledge or encumbrance, to allow the transferring Shareholder to retain all voting rights held by him immediately before the transfer. No transfer of the Shares shall be made after the end of the sixty (60) day period, nor shall any change in the terms of transfer be permitted without a new notice of intention to transfer and compliance with the requirements of this Paragraph.

2.2<u>Transfer on Death</u>.   Upon the death of any Shareholder, his personal representative (the "Representative"), immediately upon his qualification, shall serve upon the Corporation a written notice of the death of such Shareholder specifying the number of Shares which the deceased Shareholder owned at the date of death, and also specifying the terms of the will of the deceased Shareholder insofar as such will affects the testamentary disposition of the Shares, or, if the deceased Shareholder leaves no will, the identity of the deceased Shareholder's heirs under the laws of interstate succession then in effect in the state in which the deceased Shareholder's estate is subject to probate.

The Corporation shall have the option, for a period ending thirty (30) days following its receipt of said notice, to purchase all or any part of the Shares owned by the decedent, at the price and on the terms and conditions provided in Paragraphs 5 and 6 of this Agreement.   The option shall be exercised by giving written notice thereof to the decedent's estate or other successor in interest.   If the option is not exercised within the thirty (30) day period as to all Shares owned by the decedent, the Representative shall immediately serve notice in the same form as the notice given to the Corporation to the remaining Shareholders, who for a period of fifteen (15) days following their receipt of the notice shall have the option to purchase all or any part of the remaining Shares owned by the decedent, at the price and on the terms provided in this Agreement.   The option shall be exercised by giving notice thereof to the decedent's estate or other successor in interest stating the number of Shares as to which it is to be exercised.   If notices of exercise from the surviving Shareholders specify in the aggregate more Shares than are available for purchase by such Shareholders, each such Shareholder shall have priority, up to the number of shares specified in his notice, to purchase such proportion of those available Shares as the number of Shares owned by him bears to the total number of Shares owned by all Shareholders electing to purchase.   Any Shares not purchased on such a priority basis shall be allocated in one or more successive allocations to those Shareholders electing to purchase more than the number of Shares as to which they have a priority right, up to the number of Shares specified in their respective notices, in the same proportion as the number of Shares owned by each of them bears to the total number of Shares in excess of those as to which they have a priority right. In the event this option is not exercised as to all of the Shares owned by the decedent, his estate may hold and/or dispose of the remaining Shares as provided in the decedent's will or by law but all of such Shares, whether held by the estate or any distributee thereof, will remain subject to the terms and conditions of this Agreement.

2.3 <u>Removal From Office</u>.　If (a) _____, _____ and _____ are removed from their respective offices held on the date hereof by action of the Board of Directors during any time period during which the Corporation's stock issued to _____ is outstanding, and (b) _____ does not consent to such removal (with a vote by _____ as a director for such removal to be deemed a consent), then the Corporation and the remaining Shareholders shall have the option for a period of sixty (60) days following such removal, to purchase all (but not less than all) of the Shares owned by _____.　The purchase price for such Shares, which shall be paid in full in cash, shall be the sum of (i) _____ ($_____), plus (ii) _____ percent (___%) thereon compounded annually. Notice of exercise of such option shall be given to _____.　Such option shall be exercisable first by the Corporation and thereafter by the remaining Shareholders, and the method of exercise of such option shall be the same as is provided in Paragraph 2.2 of this Agreement to apply in the event of death.　In the event such option is not exercised as to all the Shares owned by _____, during the sixty (60) day period above specified, such option shall automatically expire in its entirety.　This Paragraph shall have no force or effect after the Corporation redeems all of the Corporation's stock issued to _____.

2.4 Other Events.

(a) Involuntary Dissolution. If any Shareholder attempts in any manner whatsoever to dissolve the Corporation without the consent of all Shareholders subject to this Agreement; or

(b) Bankruptcy. In the event any Shareholder is adjudicated a bankrupt (voluntary or involuntary), or makes an assignment for the benefit of his creditors; or

(c) Divorce, Separation. In the event any Shares in the Corporation are transferred or awarded to the spouse of a Shareholder under a decree of divorce or judgment of dissolution or separate maintenance, or under a property settlement or separation agreement; or

(d) Other Transfers. If any other events should occur that, were it not for the provisions of this Agreement, any Shares or any part of the Shareholder's interest therein would be sold, assigned, or otherwise transferred, voluntarily or involuntarily, under circumstances that would not bring the transfer within any other paragraph of this Agreement; then the Corporation and the remaining Shareholders shall have the option following notice of any such event(s), to purchase all or any part of the Shares owned by such Shareholder. Notice of exercise of the option shall be given to such Shareholder or his Representative. The option shall be exercisable first by the Corporation and thereafter by the remaining Shareholders, and the price, duration, terms or purchase, and method of exercise of the option shall be the same as are provided in Paragraph 2.2 of this Agreement to apply in the event of death. In the event this option is not exercised as to all the Shares owned by such Shareholder, such Shareholder or his successor in interest will hold the remaining Shares subject to the provisions of this Agreement.

(e) <u>Involuntary Transfers</u>.   No involuntary transfer, sale or other disposition of any Shares, whether by operation of law, pursuant to a security agreement, or otherwise, and including but not limited to, a transfer to a trustee in bankruptcy, receiver, purchaser at any sale under execution of any legal process, or assignee for the benefit of creditors, shall be valid or effective for any purpose whatsoever unless the transferee of such Shares (the "Transferee" herein) serves upon the Corporation written notice of such transfer stating the nature of the transfer and the number of Shares transferred or to be transferred.   On receipt of such notice, the Corporation and the remaining Shareholders shall have the option to purchase all or any part of the Shares subject to the involuntary transfer. The option shall be exercisable first by the Corporation and thereafter by the remaining Shareholders, and the price, duration, terms of purchase, and method of exercise of the option shall be the same as are provided in Paragraph 2.2 of this Agreement to apply in the event of death. In the event this option is not exercised as to all of the Shares subject to the involuntary transfer, the Transferee will hold the remaining Shares subject to the provisions of this Agreement.

3.   <u>REPURCHASE RESTRICTIONS IMPOSED BY LAW</u>. The Corporation's right to exercise any option provided for herein shall be subject to the restrictions governing the right of a corporation to purchase its own stock as set forth in Sections 500 <u>et seq</u>. of the California General Corporation Law, or its successor, and such other pertinent governmental restrictions as may now or hereafter be effective. The Corporation shall promptly take such action as may be within its powers to enable it to purchase lawfully all of the Shares which it otherwise elects to purchase including, without limitation, a recapitalization of the Corporation, a reappraisal of its assets, or any combination of the foregoing.

4. INSURANCE ON LIVES OF SHAREHOLDERS.

The Corporation may, at the exclusive discretion of its Board of Directors, purchase and maintain in effect insurance on the lives of the Shareholders, or any of them, for the purpose of providing funds which will enable the Corporation to purchase part or all of the Shares owned by any deceased Shareholder at the time of his Death. Any insurance policy or policies purchased and maintained by the Corporation for this purpose shall be designated as "Stock Purchase Funding Policies" by a duly adopted resolution of the Corporation's Board of Directors. Each Shareholder agrees that he will cooperate with the Corporation in all reasonable respects to enable the Corporation to purchase such insurance on his life, including, but not limited to, submitted to physical examinations required by insurance companies for the purpose of obtaining the insurance.

Any insurance company from which the Corporation may purchase insurance on the life of any Shareholder:

(a) shall not be deemed to be a party to this Agreement for any purpose nor in any way be responsible for its validity;

(b) shall not be obligated to inquire as to the distribution of any monies paid by it under any policy on the life of any of the Shareholders issued to the Corporation as owner; and

(c) shall be fully discharged from any and all liability under the terms of any policy issued by it which is subject to the terms of this Agreement upon payment or other performance of its obligations in accordance with the terms of such policy.

If, at any time during the life of any Shareholder whose life has been insured pursuant to policies designated as Stock Purchase Funding Policies, the Corporation becomes entitled to exercise any option to purchase Shares owned by such Shareholder, the Corporation may, in its discretion, surrender any Stock Purchase funding Policy insuring the life of such Shareholder for the interpolated terminal reserve value thereof, or exercise any other option arising under said policy, including but not limited to, the option to borrow all or any part of the interpolated terminal reserve value thereof, and may use the proceeds therefrom to exercise the option over all or any part of the Shares over which the Corporation's option extends; provided, however, if the Corporation and/or the other Shareholders elect to purchase all of the Shares owned by such Shareholder, he shall have the right but not the obligation, to purchase from the Corporation the Stock Purchase Funding Policy on his life at its interpolated terminal reserve value as of the date the Corporation received notice of the event giving rise to the purchase and sale option under this Agreement increased by the proportionate part of the gross premium last paid which covers the period beyond the notice date. The purchase price shall be paid by such Shareholder in cash prior to the closing date determined under Paragraph 5 of this Agreement or, if the Corporation elects to purchase all or any part of the Shares, the price may be set-off against the amount due such Shareholder under this Agreement.

Upon the death of any Shareholder whose life has been insured by the Corporation under any Stock Purchase Funding Policy, the Corporation shall use as much of the proceeds of such insurance as may be necessary to purchase the decedent's Shares, in accordance with Paragraph 5 hereof.

Nothing set forth herein shall be construed as requiring the Corporation to purchase and/or maintain any Stock Purchase Funding Policies, or to purchase and/or maintain Stock Purchase Funding Policies of an equal aggregate face value for each Shareholder, or to purchase and/or maintain Stock Purchase Funding Policies upon the lives of each Shareholder, nor shall the Corporation be precluded from revoking by a duly adopted resolution of its Board of Directors any designation of any insurance policies as Stock Purchase Funding Policies or cancelling or permitting the lapse of any such policies, nor shall the Corporation be precluded from purchasing and naming itself or any other person or entity as beneficiary of any insurance policies upon the lives of any of the Shareholders which are not designated by its Board of Directors as Stock Purchase Funding Policies.

5. PURCHASE PRICE

When any option to purchase Shares arises under this Agreement, except as provided in Section 2 hereof, the purchase price for such Shares shall be determined as follows:

5.1 By Agreement. When any option to purchase Shares arises hereunder, except as provided in Paragraphs 2.1 and 2.3 hereof and subject to satisfaction of the conditions precedent set forth in Paragraph 2.6 of this Agreement, the transferring Shareholder, the transferee or the Representative, as the case may be, and the Corporation and/or the Shareholders desiring to purchase the Shares shall attempt to agree upon a purchase price for such Shares within thirty (30) days following the date on which such option arises hereunder.

5.2 Appraisal if No Agreement. If the above parties are unable to agree upon a purchase price within the time specified above, the parties shall agree upon an appraiser to value the Shares. If no agreement can be reached upon an appraiser, the Corporation (on its own behalf and on behalf of each Shareholder electing to purchase Shares) shall choose one appraiser and the transferring Shareholder, the transferee, or the Representative, as the case may require, shall choose one such appraiser, and the two appraisers so chosen shall choose a third appraiser. The decision of a majority of the appraisers as to the purchase price for the Shares shall be final and binding upon all parties and may be specifically enforced by legal proceedings. Each party shall compensate the appraiser appointed by him, and the compensation of the third appraiser and the expenses of appraisal shall be borne equally by the respective parties. The portion of such compensation and fees allocated to the Corporation and the Shareholders electing to purchase the Shares shall be apportioned on a pro rata basis to the number of Shares purchased by the Corporation and each such Shareholder, respectively.

5.3 Factors Taken Into Account. In making the appraisal, the appraiser(s) shall value real estate and improvements at fair market value; machinery and equipment shall be valued at replacement cost or fair market value, whichever is lower; finished inventory shall be valued at cost or market, whichever is lower; goods in process shall be valued at cost, using the cost accounting procedures customarily employed by the Corporation in preparing its financial statements; receivables shall be valued at their fact amount, less an allowance for uncollectible items that is reasonable in view of the past experience of the Corporation and a recent review of their collectibility; all liabilities shall be deducted at their face value, and a reserve for contingent liabilities shall be established, if appropriate. The value of other comparable companies, if known, shall also be considered.

In no event shall the purchase price determined either through agreement of the parties, or through appraisal, be less than the net book value of such Shares.

6.   PAYMENT OF PURCHASE PRICE.

6.1 Payment By Corporation. Except as hereinafter provided, the purchase price payable by the Corporation shall be paid entirely in cash. In the event of the death of a Shareholder whose life has been insured by this Corporation under a Stock Purchase Funding Policy, the purchase price shall be paid in cash to the full extent of any insurance proceeds received by the Corporation, and any balance remaining shall also be paid in cash.

   6.2<u>Payment By Shareholders</u>.   In the event the Corporation does not purchase all of the Shares which it has the option to purchase and the other Shareholder(s) elect to purchase any or all of the Shares offered in accordance with this Agreement, the purchase price payable by such Shareholder(s) shall be paid entirely in cash.

7.   <u>CONSUMMATION OF SALE</u>.

   Unless the parties involved mutually agree on some other date and/or time and/or place, delivery to the Corporation and/or the Shareholders of the share certificates representing the Shares to be sold pursuant to this Agreement and payment of the purchase price therefor shall take place at a closing to be held at the principal office of the Corporation at _____ a.m. within thirty (30) days after the service of notice of the exercise of any option to purchase described in Paragraph 2 hereof or upon receipt by the Corporation of proceeds from insurance purchased in accordance with Paragraph 4 hereof, whichever is later.   At such closing, the selling Shareholder or the personal representative of a Shareholder, or the transferee, as the case may be shall deliver to the Corporation and/or the Shareholders electing to purchase Shares all share certificates representing the Shares to be purchased, duly endorsed in blank, and shall deliver, in addition, any other documents reasonably requested by the Corporation and/or such Shareholders to effectuate the purposes of this Agreement.

8.   TRANSFERS SUBJECT TO THIS AGREEMENT.

Notwithstanding the failure of the Corporation or the other Shareholders to purchase any Shares offered or the failure of the Corporation or the other Shareholders to pay the full purchase price for Shares at the times and in the manner hereinabove specified, all of the Shares shall remain at all times subject to each of the provisions of this Agreement, it being the purpose and intent of the parties hereto that all such provisions shall apply to all of the Shares whensoever, howsoever, and by whomsoever acquired, in the hands of all holders or owners, including without limitation, the parties hereto and any subsequent purchasers, transferees, or encumbrances, and whether acquired through voluntary or involuntary action, testamentary disposition, inheritance, gift, bankruptcy, operation of law, seizure and sale by legal process, or otherwise, and whether the Shares are now or hereafter issued or authorized, all such holders or owners to have the same obligations as the Shareholders. Any and all subsequent purchasers, transferees, encumbrancers, or other persons whomsoever acquiring the Shares shall be required to deliver to the Corporation an instrument in form and substance satisfactory to the Corporation accepting and agreeing to be bound by all of the terms of this Agreement.

9.   ENDORSEMENT OF SHARE CERTIFICATE.

Each of the certificates representing the Shares, or any of them, which are the subject of this Agreement, shall have endorsed on them the following words:

> None of the Shares represented by this certificate may be sold, assigned, transferred, pledged, hypothecated or in any other way disposed of or encumbered, voluntarily or involuntarily, by gift, bankruptcy, operation of law, winding up of a corporation or otherwise, nor may a proxy (revocable or irrevocable) with respect to the voting thereof by granted, except in accordance with the provisions of a Buy-Sell Agreement dated _____, 198__, a copy of which may be inspected at the principal office of this Corporation and all of the provisions of which are incorporated herein.

A copy of this Agreement shall be delivered to the Secretary of the Corporation and shall be shown by him to any person making inquiry concerning it.

10. ENFORCEMENT.

The transfer restrictions of this Agreement shall be deemed to be of the essence of the ownership of Shares. Upon application to any court of competent jurisdiction, the Corporation shall be entitled to a decree against any person violating or about to violate the provisions herein, requiring specific performance of any of the provisions herein, including those requiring a Shareholder to sell his Shares, or any part thereof to the Corporation or prohibiting a transfer or disposition of the Shares in violation hereof.

11. RECAPITALIZATIONS.

In the event the Corporation is a party to any reorganization, recapitalization, reclassification, readjustment or other change in its capital structure wherein any other stock or securities of the Corporation are to be issued in respect of all or part of the Shares of a Shareholder, then such other stock or securities shall likewise be subject to all of the terms and provisions of this Agreement.

12. TERMINATION OF AGREEMENT.

This Agreement shall terminate, and the certificates representing the Shares and any insurance policies subject to this Agreement shall be released from the terms of this Agreement upon the following events:

(a) the liquidation and dissolution of the Corporation; or

(b) the written agreement of the Corporation and the Shareholders then bound by the terms of this Agreement; or

(c) the bankruptcy or receivership of the Corporation; or

(d) the first sale of the Corporation's common stock to the public pursuant to a registration statement filed by the Corporation pursuant to the Securities Act of 1933, as amended and declared effective by the Securities and Exchange Commission; or (e)at such time as there is only one remaining Shareholder of the Corporation.

However, the termination of this Agreement shall not affect or diminish any obligations of the parties hereto to pay for any Shares actually purchased prior to such termination. Upon the termination of this Agreement for any of the above reasons, the certificates of stock held by each Shareholder shall be surrendered to the Corporation, and the Corporation shall issue new certificates for the same number of Shares but without the endorsement required by Paragraph 9 of this Agreement.

13. SERVICE BY NOTICE.

All notices or demands of any kind which may be required to be served under the terms of this Agreement shall be in writing and shall be served by personal service or by leaving a copy of such notice or demand addressed to the person to be served at the addresses of the parties set forth below opposite their respective signatures to this Agreement, whereupon service shall be deemed complete, or by mailing a copy thereof by certified or registered mail, postage prepaid, with return receipt requested.

14. GENERAL PROVISIONS.

14.1   Waiver. No waiver of any provisions of this Agreement in any instance shall be or for any purpose be deemed to be a waiver of the right of any party hereto to enforce strict compliance with the provisions hereof in any subsequent instance.

14.2   Agreement to Perform Necessary Acts. Each party hereto and the heirs, executors or administrators of the Shareholders shall perform any further acts and execute and deliver any documents or procure any court orders which may reasonably be necessary to carry out the provisions of this Agreement.

14.3   <u>Litigation and Attorneys' Fees</u>. In the event of any litigation between the parties hereto to enforce any provision or right hereunder, the unsuccessful party to such litigation covenants and agrees to pay to the prevailing party therein all costs and expenses expressly including, but not limited to, reasonably attorneys' fees and costs; expenses and attorneys' fees shall be included in and as a part of any judgment rendered in such litigation.

14.4   <u>Modification</u>. This Agreement may not be modified or amended except by a writing signed by the Shareholders and by an officer duly authorized to act on behalf of the Corporation.

14.5   <u>Counterparts</u>. This Agreement may be executed in multiple counterparts, subject to the execution of at least one of such counterparts by each of the parties hereinafter named.

14.6   <u>Testamentary Provisions</u>. Each Shareholder shall insert in his Will a direction and authorization to his Executor to fulfill and comply with the provisions hereof, and to sell the Shares in accordance herewith.

14.7   <u>Severability</u>. Every provision and part thereof of this Agreement is intended to be severable and if any term or all or part of any provision hereof is held by judicial decision to be invalid, such invalidity shall not effect the validity of the remainder of this Agreement.

14.8   <u>Offset Privilege</u>. Any monetary obligation owing from the Corporation to any Shareholder hereunder may be offset by the Corporation against any monetary obligation then owing from the Shareholder to the Corporation.

14.9   <u>Entire Agreement</u>. This Agreement is intended by the parties hereto as a final expression of their agreement and understanding with respect to the subject matter hereof and as a complete and exclusive statement of the terms thereof and supersedes any and all prior and contemporary agreements and understandings. This Agreement may not be modified or amended except by a writing signed by the Shareholders and by an officer duly authorized to act on behalf of the Corporation.

       14.10   Governing Law. This Agreement shall be construed and interpreted in accordance with the laws of the State of California.

       14.11   Paragraph Headings. The headings of the several paragraphs of this Agreement are inserted solely for convenience of reference and are not a part of and are not intended to govern, limit or aid in the construction of any term or provision hereof.

       14.12   Construction.   When   necessary,   the masculine shall include the feminine or neuter and the singular shall include the plural and vice versa.

       14.13   Binding Effect. This Agreement shall be binding upon and shall inure to the benefit of the parties hereto and their respective heirs, legal representatives, successors and assigns.

       IN WITNESS WHEREOF, the parties hereto have executed this Agreement the day and year first hereinabove written.

SHAREHOLDERS   ADDRESSES:

JOINT VENTURES

It is not unusual for parties to enter into a joint venture rather than form a corporation if the purpose of their business relationship is to accomplish a single objective or goal. A joint venture relationship is similar to a partnership and the extent of the relationship, as well as the rights and duties of the parties should be formalized in a joint venture agreement. A joint venture is taxed as a partnership because all income and loss is passed directly to the members of the joint venture. In addition, a joint venture does not require any of the formalities or maintenance of a corporation, nor does it afford the limited liability protections to the venturers.

A joint venture agreement needs to reflect the business relationship and must, therefore, be tailored to the particular needs of the members of the joint venture. The following sample document contains generic provisions as they relate to a joint venture formed for purposes of the acquisition and development of real estate and is intended to provide some guidance in the types of provisions which may be included in a real estate joint venture agreement.

SAMPLE

JOINT VENTURE AGREEMENT

THIS AGREEMENT is made as of the ____ day of _____, 19__, between _____, a California corporation, ("_____"), and _____, a _____ ("_____"), and is entered into with reference to the following facts:

RECITALS

A. _____ is in the process of acquiring fee title to that certain real property located at _____ ("Property"), the legal description of which is attached hereto as Exhibit "A" and made a part hereof by reference.

B. _____ and _____ desire to form and participate in a joint venture for the ownership, management, development, and leasing of the Property.

THEREFORE, in consideration of the mutual covenants herein set forth, the parties agrees as follows:

AGREEMENT

1. <u>FORMATION OF JOINT VENTURE</u>.

1.1<u>Formation of Joint Venture.</u>

(a) _____ and _____ hereby enter into and form a joint venture (the "Joint Venture") for the limited purposes and scope set forth herein _____ ' and _____ are sometimes referred to herein collectively as "Venturers" and individually as "Venturer".

(b) Except as expressly provided to the contrary in this Agreement, the rights and obligations of the Venturers and the administration and termination of the Joint Venture shall be governed by the California Uniform Partnership Act (California Corporations Code Section 15001 et seq.). A Venturer's interest in the Joint Venture shall be deemed personal property for all purposes. All real and other property owned by the Joint Venture shall be deemed owned by the Joint Venture as an entity, and neither Venturer, individually, shall have any ownership interest in such property.

1.2 <u>Purposes and Scope of Joint Venture.</u>

(a) _____ hereby assigns to the Joint Venture all right, title and interest of _____ in and to escrow number _____ with _____.

(b) The purpose of the Joint Venture shall be limited strictly to (i) the ownership of the Property for investment purposes; (ii) the management, development, and leasing of the Property for industrial and commercial purposes; and (iii) the ultimate sale of the Property in bulk or in part. These purposes shall not be extended by implication or otherwise except by a written agreement signed by the Venturers.

(c) Except as expressly provided herein, nothing in this Agreement shall be deemed to restrict in any way the freedom of either Venturer hereto to conduct any other business or activity whatsoever, including without limitation the acquisition, development, lease or sale of real property, without any accountability to the Joint Venture or to the other Venturer, even if such business or activity competes with the business of the Joint Venture.

1.3 Name of Joint Venture.

The business and affairs of the Joint Venture shall be conducted solely under the name of "_____" and such name shall be used at all times in connection with the Joint Venture business and affairs.

1.4 Fictitious Name Certificate.

The Venturers shall duly sign and cause to be filed and published a Fictitious Business Name Statement in connection with the formation and operation of the Joint Venture.

1.5 Scope of Venturers' Authority.

Except as otherwise expressly provided to the contrary in this Agreement, neither of the Venturers shall have any authority to act for, or to assume or agree to any obligation or responsibility on behalf of, the other Venturer of the Joint Venture. However, either Venturer is authorized to act on behalf of and bind the Joint Venture, so long as all such acts are within the provisions of Paragraph 2 of this Agreement.

1.6 Principal Place of Business.

The principal place of business of the Joint Venture shall be at the following address, or at such other address as may be mutually agreed on by both Venturers:

_____

_____

_____

_____

1.7<u>Statement of Joint Venture.</u>

The Venturers shall duly sign and cause to be filed and recorded in the office of the county recorder of the county of the principal place of business of the Joint Venture and in each county in which the Joint Venture owns real property, a Statement of Joint Venture pursuant to Section 20002 of the California Corporations Code.

2.   MANAGEMENT OF JOINT VENTURE.

2.1<u>Management of the Joint Venture Business.</u>

(a) Subject to the provisions of Paragraph 2.3 ("Budgets"), no act shall be taken or sum expended or obligation incurred by the Joint Venture or any Venturer with respect to a matter within the scope of any of the Major Decisions affecting the Joint Venture, as defined below, unless that Major Decision has been mutually approved and confirmed in writing by both Venturers. The Major Decisions shall include all decisions dealing with the following subjects:

(i)   Development of the Property or any portion thereof;

(ii) Leasing and marketing of the Property or any portion thereof;

(iii) Financing of the operations of the Joint Venture;

(iv) Selecting depreciation and accounting methods (subject to _____ 's rights under Paragraph 2.2(b)(ii)) and making other decisions with respect to treatment of various transactions for federal and state income tax purposes;

(v) Distributions of cash or property to the Venturers;

(vi) Approval of budgets;

(vii) Any expenditures or obligations incurred by or on behalf of the Joint Venture involving a sum in excess of_____ ($_____) (or such other sum as may be designated in writing by both Venturers from time to time) for any transaction or group of similar transactions, except for expenditures made and obligations incurred pursuant to a budget or development plan previously approved by both Venturers as provided in this Agreement;

(viii) Transferring, compromising or releasing any claim of the Venture except on payment in full;

(ix) Any other decision or action which by any provision of this Agreement is expressly required to be approved by both Venturers or which, considered prior to the making of such decision or the taking of such action, would be reasonably expected to have a material effect on the Joint Venture or the assets or operations thereof.

(b) If the Venturers cannot reach a decision as to any subject to be decided on by both of them so that an impasse is created in the Venture's business with respect to all or any portion of the Property, either Venturer may invoke the buy-sell procedures of Paragraph 6.5, and (if applicable) the provisions of Paragraph 2.1(c) shall also apply. From the date an impasse of the type described above is declared in a notice by either Venturer to the other Venturer, the Venturer giving such notice shall within fifteen (15) days after giving that notice institute the buy-sell procedures of Paragraph 6.5 of this Agreement. If that Venturer does not institute the provisions of that paragraph by giving to the other Venturer within that fifteen (15) day period the offer to purchase described in Paragraph 6.5, the impasse shall be deemed to have been resolved in favor of the other Venturer.

(c) When an impasse described in Section 2.1(b) is created either over a question of whether to obtain additional money for the Joint Venture or over a question of whether the Venture should spend money, upon the buy-sell procedures being instituted under Paragraph 2.1(b) as a result of the impasse, either Venturer may immediately loan to the Joint Venture all or a portion of the amount of money in controversy. This loan will be made on the following terms and conditions:

(i) The Venturer making that loan ("Lending Party") is hereby granted a security interest in all of the assets of the Joint Venture to secure repayment of the loan, and shall receive annually from the Venture interest on the unpaid balance thereof at ten percent (10%) per annum. The capital account of the other Venturer ("Non-lending Party") shall be debited for this interest. The Venture shall sign all documents, including without limitation a UCC-1 financing statement, reasonably requested by the Lending Party to perfect the security interest granted hereunder. Notwithstanding any other provision of this Agreement, the allocation of this interest expense for purposes of determining taxable income or loss shall be consistent with the provisions of this Paragraph 2.1(c)(i).

(ii) For so long as all or any part of the loan remains unrepaid to the Lending Party (but in no event longer than the buy-sell period as instituted under Paragraph 2.1(b), the Lending Party's capital account shall be credited with one hundred percent (100%) of all profits and losses (as determined by the independent certified public accountant described in Paragraph 2.2(b)(v)) earned by the Joint Venture during the period that loan remains so unpaid. This provision shall not, however, impair the Non-lending Party's right to share in the remaining profits which are generated by liquidation of the Venture as provided for in this Agreement. Notwithstanding the provisions of this Paragraph 2.1(c)(ii), the money paid under Paragraph 2.1(c) shall at all other times be treated as a loan to the Joint Venture and shall otherwise be subject to the provisions of Paragraph 3.3(b)(i) (relating to repayment of loans).

(iii) If the Non-lending Party is the Managing Partner (described in Paragraph 2.2), its status as such may be terminated at the sole option of the Lending Party, which may substitute itself as Managing Partner until this loan has been repaid in full. In no event during the buy-sell period, once instituted under Paragraph 2.1(b), shall the Managing Partner have the right to sell any portion of the Property which was not subject to sell at the time the loan under this Paragraph 2.1(c) was made.

2.2<u>Duties and Compensation of Managing Partner.</u>

(a) Except as may be provided to the contrary in this Agreement, unless and until otherwise agreed to in writing by both Venturers, _____ shall be the Venturer responsible for managing the Joint Venture affairs ("Managing Partner"). Subject to the provisions of Paragraph 2.1, the Managing Partner will be responsible for the day-to-day business operations of the Venture, and shall have the power to sign, on behalf of the Venture, all documents necessary for the management of the business, except that all loan documents, leases, and conveyances shall be signed by both Venturers.

(b) _____ hereby accepts appointment as Managing Partner and agrees to use his best efforts to discharge or cause the discharge of the duties of Managing Partner under this Agreement. Subject to the provisions of Paragraphs 2.1 and 2.2(c), the Managing Partner shall implement or cause to be implemented all Major Decisions approved by the Venturers and shall conduct or cause to be conducted, at the expense of the Joint Venture, the day-to-day ordinary and usual business and affairs of the Joint Venture in accordance with and as limited by this Agreement, including without limitation the following.

(i) Provide the development expertise necessary to process all applications for approvals required to develop the Property, to proceed with the development of the Property in accordance with development plans approved by the Venturers, and to generally carry forward and do everything necessary to complete the development substantially according to such approved plans and according to such amendments thereto as shall be agreed on from time to time by the parties;

(ii) Supervise all accounting services, including the payment of suppliers, contractors and subtrades, payroll, and maintenance of all books of account and financial records in connection with the activities of the Joint Venture and to provide all such other accounting and bookkeeping services as may be necessary or appropriate in fully documenting and recording the business of the Joint Venture and development and ownership of the Property, provided, however, that all accounting methods and procedures for the Joint Venture shall be subject to _____ prior approval, and provided further that _____ shall have the right, as an expense of the Joint Venture, to prepare and maintain all books of account and financial, accounting, and tax returns and records of the Joint Venture;

(iii) To the extent that money is available therefor, pay, before delinquency and before the addition thereto of interest or penalties, all taxes, assessments, rents and other impositions applicable to the Property and the development thereof;

(iv) Negotiate and enter into and supervise the performance of contracts covering the development of the Property and the making of any repairs or alterations thereto (providing all such contracts are within ten percent (10%) of a budget item to which those contracts relate, which budget item has been approved by the Venturers), and no such contract may be modified, amended or terminated until approved by both Venturers if that contract, when originally entered into or modified, required this approval of both Venturers;

(v) Subject to _____ rights under Paragraph 2.2(b)(ii), supervise or otherwise provide for the preparation of an annual return for the Joint Venture by an independent certified public accountant to be agreed on by the Venturers and permit either Venturer, or any person designated by a Venturer, at any reasonable time to audit the books, records and accounts of the Management Partner relating to the Property and the development and ownership thereof;

(vi) Prepare and deliver to each Venturer quarterly reports of the state of the development of the Property, which reports shall include at least an operating statement comparing current operating expenses to the budget and any other factors of significance with respect to the activities of the Joint Venture;

(vii) Retain or employ and coordinate the services of all employees, independent contractors, architects, engineers, accountants, lawyers, leasing agents, property managers, and other persons and entities necessary or appropriate to carry out the development, and the operation following completion of development, of the Property, subject to the prior approval of both Venturers;

(viii) Timely pay, to the extent that funds are available therefor, all insurance premiums, debts and other obligations and budget items which have had the prior approval of the Venturers as provided under this Agreement;

(ix) Maintain all funds paid by the parties in connection with the development of the Property in an account or accounts in a bank or banks approved by the Venturers;

(x) Make, when permitted or required by this Agreement, periodic distributions of cash or property to the parties in accordance with the provisions of this Agreement;

(xi) Comply promptly with all present and future laws, ordinances, rules, regulations and requirements of all federal, state, county, city or other governmental or quasi-governmental agencies which may be applicable to the Property or to the development, ownership or operation thereof;

(xii) Perform all other obligations provided elsewhere in this Agreement to be performed by the Managing Partner;

(xiii) Supervise matters coming within the terms of this Agreement, including the direct inspection and supervision of all design, planning, development, construction, improvement, repair, alteration or other activity in connection with the development of the Property, and to make final inspections of all completed work and to approve bills previously budgeted for payment;

(xiv)   Actively seek sound tenants for, and to supervise and participate in negotiating the leasing or, all space available for lease on the Property, and in this regard to hire and actively supervise leasing agents for the Property on behalf of the Joint Venture;

(xv) Maintain, manage and operate the Property and the development thereof in an efficient manner and to ensure that the effective and expeditious carrying out of all duties, obligations and functions of the Managing Partner to the best interest and benefit of the Joint Venture.

(c) Notwithstanding any provision of this Agreement to the contrary, except for expenditures made and obligations incurred which have been previously approved by both Venturers, or which are directly pursuant to a budget item approved by both Venturers or which are otherwise not required by the terms of this Agreement to be approved by the parties, the Managing Partner shall not have any authority to make any expenditure or incur any obligations with respect to the Property or the development thereof.

(d) The Managing Partner shall be entitled to reimbursement of reasonable costs and expenses necessarily paid by it from its own funds in its management of the Joint Venture business, as well as advances made for the Joint Venture's account, so long as such costs, expenses and advances are within the approved budgets described in Paragraph 2.3.

2.3 <u>Budgets</u>.

At least quarterly, the Managing Partner shall prepare and submit for consideration and approval by both Venturers a budget setting forth the estimated capital, operating and other expenditures required in connection with, and estimated receipts from, the activities of the Joint Venture for the period covered by the budget. When approved in writing by the Venturers, the Managing Partner shall implement the budget and shall be authorized, subject to the requirements of Paragraph 2.2(c), without the need for further approval by the parties, to make the expenditures and to incur the obligations provided for in the budget.

2.4 <u>Contracts with Related Parties</u>.

The Managing Partner shall not enter into any contract, agreement, lease or other arrangement for the furnishing to or the Joint Venture of goods, services or space with any party or entity related to, or affiliated by direct or indirect ownership or profit participation with, any Venturer or with respect to which any Venturer or partner or offices of a Venturer or any party or entity related to or affiliated with any such Venturer has any direct or indirect ownership or control unless the identity and relationship of such party to the Managing Partner, together with such contract, agreement, lease or other arrangement, has been disclosed in a budget which has been approved by both Venturers.

3. <u>CONTRIBUTIONS TO CAPITAL, OWNERSHIP AND DISTRIBUTIONS</u>.

3.1 <u>Initial Capital Contributions</u>.

The parties agree to make the following initial capital contributions:

(a) As provided in Paragraph 1.2(a), _____ hereby contributes to the Joint Venture all its right, title and interest in and to the escrow described in Paragraph 1.2(a). _____ has reviewed and hereby approves the escrow documents for the sale of the Property to _____. Upon the close of the escrow, the Joint Venture shall assume all liens, encumbrances, and other matters as provided in the above escrow instructions.

(b) _____ shall obtain or otherwise provide all financing (including construction and permanent loans) reasonably necessary to fully develop the Property and shall contribute to the Venture all working capital reasonably required to operate the Property and not otherwise available from the construction or permanent loan for the Property. All capital contributed or obligations incurred by _____, including reimbursement for all costs incurred by _____ and reimbursed by in connection with acquisition of the Property (including without limitation all payments of principal and interest made prior to the conveyance of the Property to the Partnership, and all costs which pertain to the purchase money encumbrance or any other encumbrance relating directly to the acquisition or development of the Property), and all costs of those funds contributed by _____, shall be reimbursed to _____ from the proceeds of any sale or refinancing of all or any portion of the Property (after payment of current portions of debt service and normal operating costs) until such amounts are entirely reimbursed to _____. As used in this Paragraph 3.1(b), "cost of funds" shall mean _____. Capital contributions under this Paragraph 3.1(b) shall have a value equal to the amount contributed, excluding any costs of funds and sums financed by loans on the Property.

(c) As its capital contribution to the Joint Venture, _____ hereby agrees to provide all development and management services called for by the Managing Partner under this Agreement throughout the term of the Joint Venture.

3.2 <u>Interests of Parties</u>.

The parties agree that they shall have the following interests in the assets and profits of the Joint Venture and shall, to the extent the proceeds from the operation and ultimate sale of the Property are insufficient, also share in the following proportions with respect to all losses incurred in connection with the business of the Joint Venture and development of the Property pursuant to this Agreement, and that their respective ownership interest (hereinafter call "Ownership Percentage Interest") is, as of the date of this Agreement, as follows:

_____ _____%
_____ _____%
_____ _____%

3.3 <u>Distributions to Venturers</u>.

(a) At such time and in such amounts as may be decided by the Venturers, and subject to the provisions of Paragraph 3.1(b), cash distributions shall be made of funds which become available to the Joint Venture from time to time after payment of current portions of debt service and normal operating costs (hereinafter called "Distributable Funds").

(b) The Distributable Funds shall be distributed to the parties in accordance with the following priorities if those funds are received from the Venture's operation of the Property in the ordinary course of the Venture's business:

(i) First, in payment to _____ as guaranteed payment, a return on all capital contributed and costs incurred by _____ under Paragraph 3.1(b), which return shall be _____ percent (__%) per year from the date of each such contribution or cost so made or incurred, until paid;

(ii) Second, the balance of Distributable Funds, if any, shall be distributed to the parties in accordance with their respective Ownership Percentage Interest.

(c) The Distributable Funds shall be distributed to the parties in accordance with the following priorities if those funds are received by the Venture as proceeds from the sale or refinancing of the Property:

(i) First, in payment of the entire amount of principal and accrued interest on loans, if any, made to the Joint Venture, by entities or persons other than Partners, then repayment of loans, if any, by a Partner;

(ii) Second, in payment to _____ as a guaranteed payment, a return on all capital contributed and costs incurred by _____ under Paragraph 3.1(b), to the extent not previously paid under Paragraph 3.3(b)(ii), above;

(iii) Third, in payment of all positive capital account balances after the differences, if any, between all such balances have been reduced to zero as provided in Paragraph 3.3(d), below;

(iv) Fourth, the balance of Distributable Funds, if any, shall be distributed to the parties in accordance with their respective Ownership Percentage Interests.

(d) Notwithstanding the above, if _____ has a negative capital account upon the termination of the Venture, _____ shall at that time immediately contribute to the Venture cash in a sum equal to its then existing negative capital account balance.

4. TAX STATUS, ALLOCATIONS AND REPORTS.

4.1 Tax Status.

As provided in Paragraph 2.2(b)(v), the Managing Partner shall cause to be timely prepared and filed all tax returns and statements which must be filed on behalf of the Joint Venture with any taxing authority, and shall submit such returns and statements to both Venturers prior to filing.

4.2 Allocations.

For accounting and federal and state income tax purposes, except as herein otherwise specifically provided, all income, deductions, credits, gains and losses of the Joint Venture shall be allocated to the Venturers in their respective Ownership Percentage Interest. All profits and losses of the Venture shall be as determined for federal income tax purposes by the accountant for the Joint Venture.

4.3 Reports; Special Audits.

Any provision hereof to the contrary notwithstanding, solely for United States federal income tax purposes, each of the Venturers hereby recognizes that the Joint Venture will be subject to all provisions of Subchapter K of Chapter 1 of Subtitle A of the United States Internal Revenue Code of 1954, as amended; provided, however, the filing of U.S. Partnership Returns of Income shall not be construed to extend the purposes of the Joint Venture or expand the obligations or liabilities of the Venturers. At the request of either Venturer, the Joint Venture shall file an election under Section 754 of the United States Internal Revenue Code of 1954, as amended. In the event either Venturer desire an audit of the books of the Venture other than an annual audit, such audit will be paid for by the Venturer requesting it.

5. FISCAL YEAR.

The fiscal year of the Joint Venture shall end on the last day of _____ of each year unless _____ chooses to elect another fiscal year-end.

6. TERM AND TERMINATION.

6.1 Term.

The Joint Venture shall begin on the date of this Agreement first written above and shall continue for a term of forty (40) years or until the sale of the entire Property, and conversion of all assets to cash, whichever occurs sooner, unless sooner terminated and dissolved in accordance with the provisions of this Agreement; provided, however, that if _____ has not acquired the Property and contributed the Property to the Joint Venture as provided in Paragraph 1.2(a) by _____, this Agreement and the Joint Venture shall automatically terminate and shall be of no further force or effect unless otherwise mutually agreed to in writing by the Venturers before that date.

6.2 Automatic Termination.

(a) Except as expressly provided to the contrary in Paragraph 6.2(a)(vii), the Joint Venture shall automatically and immediately terminate upon the occurrence of any of the following events; the Venturer causing such termination shall be deemed the "Withdrawing Party," and any of the following events shall also constitute a default under this Agreement:

(i) If a Venturer shall file a voluntary petition in bankruptcy or shall be adjudicated a bankrupt or insolvent, or shall file any petition or answer seeking any reorganization, arrangement, composition, readjustment, liquidation, dissolution or similar relief for itself under the present or any future federal bankruptcy act or any other present or future applicable federal, state, or other statute or law relative to bankruptcy, insolvency or other relief for debtors, or shall seek or consent to or acquiesce in the appointment of any trustee, receiver, conservator or liquidator of said Venturer or of all or any substantial part of its properties or its interest in the Joint Venture; or

(ii) If a court of competent jurisdiction shall enter an order, judgment or decree appointing a trustee or receiver for a Venturer or approving a petition filed against a Venturer seeking any reorganization, arrangement, composition, readjustment, liquidation, dissolution or similar relief under the present or any future bankruptcy act, or any other present or future applicable federal, state or other statute or law relating to bankruptcy, insolvency or other relief for debts, and that Venturer shall acquiesce in the entry of such order, judgment or decree (the term "acquiesce" includes but is not limited to, failure to file a petition or motion to vacate or discharge such order, judgment or decree within ten (10) days after the entry of the order, judgment or decree) or such order, judgment or decree shall remain unvacated and unstayed for an aggregate of ninety (90) days (whether or not consecutive) from the date of entry thereof, or any trustee, receiver, conservator, or liquidator of such Venturer or all or any substantial part of its property or its interest in the Joint Venture shall be appointed without the consent of acquiescence of such Venturer and such appointment shall remain unvacated and unstayed for an aggregate of sixty (60) days (whether or not consecutive); or

(iii) If a Venturer shall admit in writing its inability to pay its debts as they mature; or

(iv) If a Venturer shall give notice to any governmental body of insolvency or pending insolvency; or

(v) If a Venturer shall have made an assignment for the benefit of creditors or take any other similar action for the protection or benefit of creditors;

(vi) Upon the termination or dissolution of a corporation or partnership or the transfer of any interest in a partnership which is a Venturer, unless all assets of the terminated or dissolved corporation or partnership are simultaneously transferred to a corporate successor of the type described in Paragraph 7.2(a); or

(vii) Upon the death or disability of any one of the Venturers ("disability" being defined as the inability of such Venturer to efficiently perform his duties under the Joint Venture for a continuous period of more than thirty (30) days due to a mental or physical disease or defect).

(b) Upon automatic termination of the Joint Venture as provided above, the Withdrawing Party shall immediately deliver to the Nonwithdrawing Party a quitclaim deed, properly executed and acknowledged, transferring all rights of the Withdrawing Party in the Property to the Nonwithdrawing Party. In order to secure this obligation, each Venturer hereby grants to the other a security interest in its right to the Property and assets of the Joint Venture under this Agreement, with the intent that each Venturer is hereby made a secured creditor of the other insofar as either Venturer's obligation to deliver a quitclaim deed or other obligation to the other Venturer is unperformed during the term of this Agreement hereunder, and each agrees to sign all documents, including without limitation UCC-1 financing statements, reasonably requested to perfect the security interest granted above.

6.3 <u>Termination for Default</u>.

(a) If a Venturer fails to perform any of its obligations hereunder, the other Venturer ("Nondefaulting Party") shall have the right to give such party ("Defaulting Party") a notice of default ("Notice of Default"). The Notice of Default shall set forth the nature of the obligation which the Defaulting Party has not performed.

(b) If, within the thirty (30) day period following the receipt of the Notice of Default, the Defaulting Party in good faith starts to perform such obligations and cure such default and thereafter prosecutes to completion with diligence and continuity the curing thereof and cures such default within a reasonable time, it shall be deemed that the Notice of Default was not given and the Defaulting Party shall lose no rights hereunder. If, within such thirty (30) day period, the Defaulting Party does not start in good faith the curing of such default or does not thereafter prosecute to completion with diligence and continuity the curing thereof, the Nondefaulting Party hereunder shall have the right to terminate this Joint Venture by giving the Defaulting Party written notice thereof. If the Joint Venture is so terminated, the Defaulting Party shall be deemed to be the "Withdrawing Party".

(c) The provisions of Paragraph 6.3(b) shall not apply to any default with respect to the payment of any sums of money by or to a Venturer, which sums of money shall be paid within fifteen (15) days after receipt of a Notice of Default with respect thereto. If such sums are not paid within such fifteen (15) day period, the Nondefaulting Party shall have the right to terminate this Joint Venture by giving the Defaulting Party written notice thereof, whereupon the Defaulting Party shall be deemed the "Withdrawing Party."

6.4 <u>Remedies of Nonwithdrawing Party</u>.

(a) In the event of a termination of the Joint Venture pursuant to the terms of this Agreement, the Nonwithdrawing Party may but need not elect one of the following alternatives, which election shall be made within ninety (90) days of termination by giving written notice thereof to the Withdrawing Party:

> (i) Institute the Buy-Sell Procedures set forth in Paragraph 6.5; or

> (ii) Purchase the entire undivided interest in the Joint Venture of the Withdrawing Party pursuant to the Appraisal Procedure set forth in Paragraph 6.6.

(b) The rights of the Nonwithdrawing Party under this Paragraph 6 shall not be the exclusive remedy of the Nonwithdrawing Party but shall be in addition to all other rights and remedies, if any, available to the Nonwithdrawing Party at law or in equity.

(c) Notwithstanding anything to the contrary contained in this Agreement, in the event of termination of the Joint

Venture as provided in this Paragraph 6, regardless of whether the Nonwithdrawing Party makes an election under either Paragraph 6.4(a)(i) or Paragraph 6.4(a)(ii), the Nonwithdrawing Party shall be allowed to continue with and complete the business and purposes of the Joint Venture (including the right to use the Venturer's name), and the Withdrawing Party shall be entitled to receive only its share of the income earned and received by the Venture to the date of such termination, plus the balance then in the Withdrawing Party's capital account, if any, and the balance of any unrepaid loans made by that Party to the Joint Venture, but less all indebtedness owed the Joint Venture from such Withdrawing Party. Twenty-five percent (25%) of the total amount due hereunder shall be paid to the Withdrawing Party as soon as feasible after termination, with the balance payable in three (3) equal annual installments thereafter, beginning one (1) year from the date on which the down payment is made, with interest at ____ percent (__%) per year on the unpaid balance thereof; provided, however, that no payments will be due hereunder until after the Nonwithdrawing Party receives from the Venture all money loaned or contributed to the business of the Venture by the Nonwithdrawing Party from the date of termination of the Joint Venture, and provided further that all debts of the Joint Venture have first been paid in full; in that event, the down payment shall be made, and the period for the installment payment shall begin to run, only after all such debts have been repaid and the Nonwithdrawing Party has been repaid all such payments made by it after termination of the Venture. In no event, however, shall the Nonwithdrawing Party be liable for any payments to the Withdrawing Party; all such payments are to be made, if at all, solely from the assets of the Joint Venture.

6.5 <u>Buy-Sell Procedures.</u>

Either Venturer ("Offeror Partner") may, at any time, offer to buy the interest of the other Venturer ("Offeree Partner") in the Joint Venture by delivering a written notice containing an offer price and all essential terms of the offer to the Offeree Partner; provided that the offer shall allow at least sixty (60) days from its delivery before the Offeree Partner has to perform the first act (other than acceptance of the offer) or pay the first amount due under the offer. The Offeree Partner shall have the option to either (i) sell its Joint Venture interest to the Offeror Partner; or (ii) buy the Offeror Partner's interest, pursuant to the terms of the original offer. Notice of the Offeree Partner's election to buy or sell shall be given in writing to the Offeror Partner within ten (10) days of receipt of the original offer. The failure to give such a notice of intent strictly in accordance with the above time limit shall be deemed an acceptance of the original offer. If either party who is the purchaser of the other party's interest under this Paragraph 6.5 does not close the purchase of that interest pursuant to the provisions of this Paragraph, that party shall be deemed to be in default hereunder, and the other party, in addition to its other rights and remedies, may (i) continue the Joint Venture business, or (ii) purchase the interest in the Joint Venture of the defaulting party at a purchase price equal to eighty percent (80%) of the purchase price at which the defaulting party had agreed to purchase the interest of the other party under the provisions of this Paragraph. All loans and cash contributions by either Partner to the Joint Venture shall be repaid simultaneously with the first payment made in connection with any agreement reached under the procedures of this Paragraph 6.5.

6.6 Appraisal Procedure.

(a) If, upon termination of the Joint Venture pursuant to Paragraph 6.2 or 6.3 hereof, the Nonwithdrawing Party elects to proceed under this Paragraph 6.6 to purchase the interest of the Withdrawing Party in and to the Joint Venture at the appraised value ("Appraised Value") thereof, it shall give the Withdrawing Party written notice thereof within thirty (30) days after such termination, and in such notice shall designate the first appraiser ("First Appraiser").

(b) Within fifteen (15) days after service of the notice referred to in Paragraph 6.6(a) above, the Withdrawing Party shall give written notice to the Nonwithdrawing Party, designating the second appraiser ("Second Appraiser"). If the Second Appraiser is not so designated within or by the time above specified, then the appointment of the Second Appraiser shall be made in the same manner as is hereinafter provided for the appointment of the Third Appraiser in a case where the First and Second Appraisers and the parties themselves are unable to agree upon the Third Appraiser. The First and Second Appraisers so designated or appointed shall meet within ten (10) days after the Second Appraiser is appointed and shall each prepare a separate appraisal; if, within thirty (30) days after the Second Appraiser is appointed, the First and Second Appraisers do not agree upon a single Appraised Value, as more fully set forth in Paragraph 6.6(c) hereof, they shall themselves appoint a Third Appraiser who shall be a competent and impartial person; and in the event of their being unable to agree upon such appointment within ten (10) days after the foregoing time, the Third Appraiser shall be selected by the parties themselves if they can agree thereon within a further period of fifteen (15) days. If the parties do not so agree, then either party, on behalf of both, may request such appointment by the Presiding Judge of the Superior Court of the State of California, County of _____. The Third Appraiser so selected or appointed shall thereafter prepare an appraisal within thirty (30) days after his selection or appointment. In the event of the failure, refusal or inability of any appraiser to act, a new appraiser shall be appointed in his stead, which appointment shall be made in the same manner as above provided for the appointment of the appraiser so failing, refusing or being unable to act. Each party shall pay the fees and expenses of the one of the two original appraisers appointed by such party or in whose stead, as above provided, such appraiser was appointed, and the fees and expenses of the Third Appraiser and all other expenses, if any, shall be borne equally by both parties. Any appraiser designated to serve in accordance with the provisions of this Agreement shall be disinterested and shall be qualified to appraise real estate of the type covered by this Agreement situated in the vicinity of the Property, and shall otherwise be qualified to appraise the Joint Venture assets.

(c) The appraisers shall each determine the Appraised Value on one hundred percent (100%) of the Joint Venture, which shall be the amount by which (i) the fair market value at the time such appraisal is made of all assets of the Joint Venture is in excess of (ii) all liabilities of the Joint Venture, including without limitation, the liabilities for repayment of all loans to the Joint Venture. As used herein, "fair market value" shall mean the value of the Property and assets for cash for the use then zoned and in the condition the Property and assets are then in as of the date of the appraisals. The average of all three appraisals (if a Third Appraiser is selected or appointed) shall be deemed to be and conclusively accepted as the Appraised Value for purposes of this Paragraph 6.

(d) The Nonwithdrawing Party shall purchase the Withdrawing Party's interest in the Joint Venture for a cash price equal to the Appraised Value multiplied by the Ownership Percentage Interest of the Withdrawing Party. The closing of such purchase shall occur at a mutually acceptable time within thirty (30) days after written notice of the decision of the appraisers has been delivered to the Venturers, and otherwise shall be conducted in accordance with Paragraph 6.4(c) hereof.

(e) If the appraisers shall fail to reach a decision within ninety (90) days after the appointment of the Third Appraiser, the Nonwithdrawing Party shall have the right to withdraw its election to purchase the Withdrawing Party's interest in the Joint Venture pursuant to this Paragraph 6.6, and shall have the right to institute the buy-sell procedures set forth in Paragraph 6.5, by giving the

Withdrawing Party written notice thereof within thirty days after the end of such ninety (90) day period.

6.7 <u>Joint Venture Liquidation Procedures</u>.

(a) Contemporaneously with the termination of the Joint Venture under this Agreement, the Joint Venture, to the extent, but only to the extent of the assets of the Joint Venture, shall pay or make provisions for the discharge of the obligations of the Joint Venture, save and except mortgage indebtedness on which no Venturer has either personal or corporate liability, and shall distribute the balance of the assets, if any, subject to such mortgage indebtedness and in a manner consistent with the other provisions of this Agreement which relate to distribution to Venturers and to termination of the Joint Venture. After the foregoing has been accomplished, it shall be deemed that the Joint Venture has been dissolved and wound up, this Agreement shall terminate, and the Venturers shall thereupon sign and cause to be recorded in the manner provided by law a Notice of Dissolution of Partnership.

(b) During the period beginning with termination of the Joint Venture pursuant hereto and ending with the winding up of its affairs and termination of this Agreement pursuant to Paragraph 6.7(a) above, the business affairs of the Joint Venture shall be conducted by the Nonwithdrawing Party as provided in Paragraph 6.4(c) so as to preserve the assets of the Joint Venture and maintain the status thereof which existed immediately prior to such termination.

7. <u>ASSIGNMENT</u>.

7.1 <u>Prohibited Transfers</u>.

Except as expressly provided for herein, no Venturer may sell, transfer, assign or otherwise transfer or mortgage, pledge, hypothecate or otherwise encumber or permit or suffer any encumbrance of all or any part of its interest in this Joint Venture unless approved, in writing, by both Venturers. Any attempt to so transfer or encumber any such interest shall be void.

7.2 Permitted Transfers.

      (a) A Venturer shall have the right, without the consent of the other Venturer, to transfer all or any part of its interest in the Joint Venture to an Affiliated Corporation as hereinafter defined. An Affiliated Corporation shall be (i) any corporation which owns fifty-one percent (51%) or more of the stock of the Venturer or (ii) any corporation, fifty-one percent (51%) or more of the stock of which is owned by the Venturer, or (iii) any corporation, fifty-one percent (51%) or more of the stock of which is owned by a shareholder who also owns at least fifty-one percent (51%) of the stock of the Venturer. After the transfer by the Venturer to an Affiliated Corporation of all of the interest of the Venturer in the Joint Venture, at the time of such transfer, all references to the Venturer in this Joint Venture shall be deemed to be a reference to such Affiliated Corporation.

      (b) In the event of any transfer or transfers permitted under this Paragraph, the interest so transferred shall be and remain subject to all of the terms and provisions of this Agreement; the assignee or transferee shall be deemed to have assumed all of the obligations hereunder relating to the interests or rights so transferred, and have such obligation jointly and severally with its transferor, unless the transferee of an interest hereunder has a net worth the same as or greater than the transferring Venturer at the time of the transfer, in which event the transferring Venturer shall be relieved of all further obligation hereunder. No change in ownership of any interest in the Venture or rights under this

Agreement shall be binding upon the other Venturer until a duplicate original copy of all instruments executed and delivered in connection with such transfer or assignment shall have been delivered to such other Venturer.

(c) Notwithstanding any other provision of this Agreement, no transfer of any interest in the Joint Venture will be permitted where that transfer could reasonably be expected to result in either (i) a termination of the Venture for tax purposes under Internal Revenue Code Section 708, or (ii) a material increase in the real property tax assessment against the Property.

8. GENERAL.

8.1 Notices.

(a) All notices, demands or requests provided for or permitted to be given pursuant to this Agreement must be in writing. All notices, demands and requests to be sent to a Venturer or any assignee of the interest of a Venturer hereunder pursuant hereto shall be given by personal delivery or by depositing the same in the United States mail, postpaid, and registered or certified, with return receipt requested, at the following address:

_____

_____

_____

_____

(b) All notices, demands and requests shall be effective upon actual receipt, whether served by personal delivery or by registered or certified United States mail, return receipt requested.

(c) By giving to the other party at least three (3) days' written notice thereof, the parties hereto and their respective successors and assigns shall have the right from time to time at any time during the term of this Agreement to change their respected addresses and each shall have the right to specify as its address any other address within the United States.

8.2 <u>Insurance</u>.

(a) The Joint Venture shall carry and maintain in force such insurance as may be decided upon by both Venturers as a Joint Venture expense, which insurance shall be so provided to the extent each Venturer is not adequately covered. Such insurance should include but not be limited to, the following insurance:

(i) Workers' Compensation insurance covering all employees of the Joint Venture in accordance with the laws of the State of California or the law of any other state in which work may be performed or services provided by the Venture. In addition to insuring statutory obligations, such coverage shall provide employers liability insurance with a limit of not less than One Million Dollars ($1,000,000.00) per occurrence.

(ii) Comprehensive general liability and automobile insurance with contractual liability, products and completed operations and broad form property damage coverage included for a limit of liability of not less than Five Million Dollars ($5,000,000.00) per occurrence combined single limit bodily injury and property damage. Completed operations coverage shall be maintained in force for a period of not less than one year after all work has been completed by, or on behalf of, the Joint Venture.

8.3 <u>Governing Law</u>.

This Agreement shall be governed by, construed and enforced in accordance with the laws of the State of California.

8.4 <u>Fees and Commissions</u>.

Each Venturer hereby represents and warrants to the other that there are no claims for brokerage or other commissions or finders or other similar fees in connection with the transactions covered by this Agreement insofar as such claims shall be based on arrangements or agreements made by or on its behalf, and each Venturer hereby agrees to indemnify and hold harmless the other from and against all liabilities, costs, damages and expenses from any such claim.

8.5 <u>Entire Agreement</u>.

This Agreement contains the entire agreement between the parties hereto relative to the formation of the Joint Venture to develop the Property. No variations, modifications or changes herein or hereof shall be binding upon any party hereto unless set forth in a document duly executed by or on behalf of such party.

8.6 <u>Waiver</u>.

No consent or waiver, expressed or implied, by any Venturer to or of any breach or default by the other Venturer in the performance by the other Venturer of its obligations hereunder shall be deemed or construed to be a consent or waiver to or of any other breach or default in the performance of such other party of the same or any other obligations of such Venturer hereunder. Failure on the part of any Venturer to complain of any act or failure to act on the part of the other Venturer or to declare the other Venturer in default, irrespective of how long such failure continues, shall not constitute a waiver of such Venturer or its rights hereunder.

8.7 Severability.

If any provision of this Agreement or the application thereof to any person or circumstance shall be invalid or unenforceable to any extent, the remainder of this Agreement and the application of such provisions to other persons or circumstances shall not be affected thereby. It shall be enforced to the greatest extent permitted by law.

8.8 Attorneys' Fees.

In the event litigation is instituted by any Venturer for the purpose of enforcing or interpreting any provision of this Agreement, the prevailing party in such litigation shall be entitled to its reasonable attorneys' fees.

8.9 Binding Agreement.

Subject to the restrictions on transfer and encumbrances set forth herein, this Agreement shall inure to the benefit of and be binding upon the undersigned Venturers and their respective successors and assigns. Whenever, in this instrument, a reference to any party or Venturer is made, such reference shall be deemed to include a reference to the successors and assigns of such Venturer.

8.10 Time of Essence.

Time is hereby expressly made of the essence with respect to the performance by parties of their respective obligations under this Agreement.

8.11 <u>Authority</u>.

Each individual signing for each of the parties hereunder warrants and represents that he is an authorized agent of such party, on whose behalf he is executing this Agreement.

8.12 <u>Further Assistance</u>.

Each party agrees to execute such other and further instruments and documents as may be necessary or proper in order to complete the transactions contemplated by this Agreement.

IN WITNESS WHEREOF, THIS AGREEMENT, is executed effective as of the date first set forth above.

By: _____, President

By: _____, President

ASSET AND STOCK SALES

As previously discussed the two following documents are for use with the sale of either the assets or the stock of an on-going business. The decision as to whether to sell or purchase stock versus assets is a complex legal question which involves numerous tax and accounting considerations. Usually, the sale of stock involves the maintenance of the on-going "selling" corporation, whereas an asset purchase results in the dissolution of the "selling" corporation. The following stock purchase and asset purchase agreements are intended to include those generic provisions appropriate to the two particular transactions. Most of the representations and warranties are standard. Various modifications and additions may be necessary depending upon the particular facts of the transaction.

SAMPLE

ASSET PURCHASE AGREEMENT

This agreement is made and entered into on the date last below written by and among _____, a California corporation (hereinafter referred to as "Buyer"), and _____, (hereinafter referred to as "Seller").

<u>RECITALS</u>

WHEREAS, Seller owns and operates a _____ (the "Business") located at _____, and operated under the name of _____; and

WHEREAS, Seller desires to sell to Buyer various assets of the Business, including without limitation furniture, fixtures and equipment, machinery, merchandise inventory, customer and supplier lists, supplies, goodwill, business, business name, stationery and advertising materials, all as more specifically provided for herein; and

WHEREAS, Buyer desires to prevent Seller from competing with Buyer and/or its successors or assigns in the operation of another competing or potentially competing business for a reasonable period of time and within a reasonable geographic area on the terms and conditions hereinafter provided.

FOR VALUABLE CONSIDERATION, the adequacy and sufficiency of which is hereby acknowledged, including without limitation the premises and the mutual covenants and promises hereinafter contained, it is hereby mutually agreed as follows:

AGREEMENT

1. <u>Agreement</u>. Seller agrees to sell, transfer and convey and Buyer agrees to purchase certain assets of the Business pursuant to the terms and conditions hereinafter set forth.

2. <u>Definitions</u>. The following terms shall have the meanings set forth below:

(a)"<u>Closing Date</u>" or "<u>Closing</u>" shall mean the time and date of the closing of the purchase and sale contemplated hereby, which shall occur within a reasonable period of time after the Execution Date as hereinafter defined. Closing is tentatively scheduled to occur on the _____ day of _____, 19___, at the hour of ___ a.m., at the offices of the Buyer at _____, or at such other place, date and hour as shall be determined by written consent of the parties or as otherwise provided herein. All matters undertaken at the Closing shall be deemed to occur simultaneously.

(b)"<u>Execution Date</u>" shall be the date of execution of this Agreement by the last executing party.

(c)"<u>Financial Statements</u>" shall mean the unaudited financial statements of the Business for the period of time ending _____, 19____ .

3. <u>Assets Purchased</u>. Seller agrees to sell, transfer, convey and deliver possession of, and Buyer, in reliance upon the covenants, representations and warranties contained herein, agrees to buy and take possession of, all on the terms and conditions stated herein, the Business owned and operated by Seller consisting of the following described assets at the prices stated herein. A listing of said assets is attached hereto as Schedule "A" and incorporated

herein by this reference.   The assets to be purchased expressly excludes any accounts receivable of the Seller.   Buyer shall not be required to take any action to collect accounts receivable with respect to the business previously owned and operated by Seller.

(a)<u>Furniture, Fixtures and Equipment</u>.   All of the furniture, commercial fixtures not constituting part of the real estate, machinery and other equipment located on the premises of the Business as shown on Schedule "A", attached hereto and incorporated herein by this reference, for a total purchase price of _____ Dollars ($_____).

(b)<u>Inventory</u>.   All of the inventory of the Business and related items on the premises of the Business at the Closing Date.   A listing of said inventory items is shown on Schedule "B", attached hereto and incorporated herein by this reference.   The total purchase price of said inventory items shall be the value thereof as determined by a physical inventory taken by both Seller (or its representatives) and Buyer based upon the "retail method" of valuing inventory wherein value is determined as a fraction of the sales prices of the various inventory items based upon Seller's normal markups for said items.   Said physical inventory shall be taken not more than _____ (_____) days prior to the Closing Date.   Seller and one or more representatives of Buyer shall be physically present.   Seller agrees that said inventory will be substantially the same in both composition and value on the Closing Date as it is on the Execution Date of this Agreement and the date of the taking of said physical inventory.   Seller represents that as of _____, 19___, using the "retail method" of valuing inventory, the value of all of the aforesaid inventory items as approximately _____ Dollars ($_____).

(c)<u>Supplies</u>. All of the stationery, advertising materials, wrapping and other supplies presently being used in connection with the operation of the business and on the premises of the Business at the Closing Date, for a total purchase price of _____ Dollars ($_____).

(d)<u>Accounts Receivable</u>. All of the accounts receivable of the business for items purchased on or before _____, 19___. The total purchase price of said accounts receivable shall be equal to the amounts due on said accounts but expressly excludes any part of said accounts that relate to purchases chases made by the Seller after _____, 19___.

(e)<u>Goodwill</u>. All of the goodwill of the business of Seller, including all customer and supplier lists and records, and including the name of the Business for a total purchase price of _____ Dollars ($_____). Buyer and/or its successors and assigns shall be entitled to use the aforesaid name and Seller agrees not to use the name of the Business or any similar name which could be reasonably confused with said name at any time after the Closing Date.

(f) <u>Covenants Not to Compete: Non-Competition by Seller</u>. For the purpose of assuring Buyer that the Business of Seller being purchased hereunder can be operated for a reasonable period of time and within a reasonable geographic area without competition from Seller for itself and for its heirs, executors, personal representatives, successors and assigns, agree that it will not within a _____ (_____) mile radius of _____ in _____ engage either individually or as a director, officer, employee, partner, or joint venturer, or as an owner of more than (_____) percent (_____) of the securities of any class of stock of any corporation that is in the business of operating a business or any other activity which is now or may in the future be in direct or indirect competition with Buyer and/or its successors or assigns, for a period of _____ (_____) years after the Closing Date. During said period of time Buyer shall pay to Seller _____ Dollars ($_____) per month for a total of _____ (_____)months. Seller agrees that the geographic area and time duration of the limitation imposed by this provision are both fair and reasonable, and acknowledge that this covenant will not constitute a limitation or handicap to Seller in securing future employment. Seller shall without the payment of any further consideration be physically present at the business location of the Business during normal business hours to assist Buyer in learning and operating the business for _____ (_____) days after the Closing Date.

(f) <u>Miscellaneous Assets</u>. For miscellaneous assets including without limitation _____ for a total purchase price of _____ ($_____).

4. <u>Total Consideration to be Paid - Asset Purchase</u>. The total consideration to be paid by Buyer to Seller pursuant to this Agreement shall be equal to the sum of _____ Dollars ($_____) to be paid at the Closing in the form of cash or a cashier's check made payable to the Seller.

The total consideration to be paid by Buyer to Seller in the amount of _____ Dollars ($_____) shall be paid as follows:

(a)_____ Dollars ($_____) as a downpayment, receipt of which is hereby acknowledged by Seller; and

(b)_____ Dollars ($_____) in cash or certified check at the Closing; and

(c) The balance shall be evidenced by a negotiable promissory note (estimated to be in the amount of _____ Dollars ($_____), subject to adjustment for inventory valuation and other adjustments. Said note shall bear interest at the rate of _____ percent (___%) per annum, shall be payable in equal monthly installments over a period of _____ (____) years, less any amounts for offsets, and shall be secured by a security interest securing payment of _____ Dollars ($_____) with regard to the furniture, fixtures, equipment, inventory, accounts receivable, customer and supplier lists, and stationery and advertising materials. Said note shall be further secured by a deed of trust securing payment of _____ Dollars ($_____) on the real estate located at _____ which is being contemporaneously sold with the assets transferred pursuant to this Agreement.

5. <u>Bulk Sales</u>. Following the mutual execution of this Agreement and at least ten (10) days prior to the Closing Date, Seller shall furnish Buyer with a list of Seller's existing creditors, signed and sworn to or affirmed by Seller or Seller's agent. Said list shall contain the names and business addresses of all creditors of Seller, both personal and business, and whether general (unsecured)

or secured, with the amounts due and owing (when known), and the names and addresses of all persons who are known to Seller to have asserted claims against Seller even though such claims are contingent or disputed. Seller and Buyer shall also prepare a schedule of the assets transferred pursuant to this Agreement in sufficient detail to identify said assets. Said list of assets is attached hereto as Schedule "C" and incorporated herein by this reference. Buyer at its option may cancel this Agreement in the event Seller fails to comply with the aforesaid requirements. Seller shall repay to Buyer and to others all sums previously paid pursuant to this Agreement. It is the intention of the parties that this provision is to allow Buyer to take such reasonable steps to comply with the bulk sales provisions of the Uniform Commercial Code. However, the failure of Buyer to take such compliance steps shall not relieve Seller in any respect from any of its obligations hereunder.

6. <u>Covenants, Representations and Warranties of Seller</u>. Seller covenants, represents, warrants and agrees as of _____, 19__, and as of the Closing Date, as follows:

(a) <u>Assets: Lawful Owner, Marketable Title</u>:

(i) <u>Lawful Owner</u>. Seller has good, sufficient and marketable title in and to all of its assets and properties being sold, transferred or assigned hereunder, including those assets listed on its Financial Statements. All assets and properties of the Seller, except as set forth in the Financial Statements, are now and will be at the Closing, free and clear of all mortgages, liens, charges, encumbrances, equities, pledges, conditional sales agreements, security agreements, options, claims or restrictions of any nature whatsoever. Seller has now and will have at the Closing good right, title and authority to sell, transfer and convey the aforesaid assets and will warrant and defend said assets against any and all claims and demands of all persons whomsoever.

(ii)   <u>UCC Searches - Personal Property</u>. Seller, on or before the Closing Date and at its own expense, shall provide Buyer with (i) evidence of ownership of all of its personal property issued by the Secretary of State of each State where the Seller owns personal property and (ii) the results of UCC searches on all personal property of the Seller to be conveyed to Buyer hereunder.

(b) <u>Corporate Standing/Authority</u>.   Seller is a corporation duly organized, validly existing and in good standing under the laws of the State of _____, has all requisite power and authority to consummate the transactions contemplated by this Agreement, has by proper corporate proceedings duly authorized the execution and delivery of this Agreement and the consummation of all transactions contemplated herein, and in any contemporaneous agreements or other agreements connected herewith.

(c) <u>Warranty of Financial Information by Seller</u>. Any and all financial information concerning Seller's business provided to Buyer including but not limited to profit and loss statements, balance sheets, position statements, income tax returns, and the like, are true and complete statements of, and fairly and accurately present the financial condition of the Seller. Said financial information was correctly and properly prepared in accordance with generally accepted accounting principles and applicable tax laws, consistently applied throughout the periods indicated. No material changes have occurred since the date such statements or tax returns were prepared or filed.

(d) <u>Payment of Debts by Seller</u>. Seller will pay or cause to be paid all debts, taxes and liabilities which are or might become a lien or charge against any of the assets to be conveyed pursuant to this Agreement.

(e) <u>Contracts</u>. Seller is not a party to nor is bound by any written or oral agreement including without limitation agreements for the purchase of materials, equipment, supplies or services (i) requiring the payment of an aggregate sum in excess of _____ Dollars ($_____), (ii) having a term continuing beyond the Closing Date or (iii) entered into outside of the ordinary course of its business.

(f) <u>No Breach of Contract</u>. Seller is not now in breach of any agreement or contract which affects the business of Seller nor is delinquent in the payment of any amount due in connection with said business. Furthermore, there are neither asserted, pending or threatened claims nor any legal basis for a claim that Seller has breached any term or condition of any agreement or commitment to which Seller is a party or by which Seller is bound. Seller has no existing contract or commitment extending beyond the Closing Date or involving payment by Seller of more than _____ Dollars ($_____) except those contracts or commitments listed in Schedule "E", a copy of which is attached hereto and incorporated herein by this reference. True and complete copies of all items listed in Schedule "E" have been or will be delivered to Buyer on or before _____, 19__. Seller has complied with and is not in default under any provisions of any contracts, instruments and commitments to which it is a party. Said contracts, instruments and commitments are valid and enforceable by Seller in accordance with their terms and conditions.

(g) <u>No Conflict With Agreements</u>. Neither the execution and delivery of this Agreement by Seller nor the consummation of the transactions contemplated hereby will, with or without the giving of notice or the passage of time, or both, (i) conflict with or result in a breach of or accelerate the maturity of any indebtedness or any obligation thereunder, (ii) create or impose any lien, charge, or encumbrance upon any of the properties or assets of

Seller, (iii) give rise to a right of termination of any material agreement or commitment of which Seller is a party or by which any of the material assets or properties of Seller are bound or affected, and (iv) conflict with or violate to the best of Seller's knowledge any judgment, decree, order, statute or other provision of law, rule or regulation of any governmental body binding upon Seller.

(h) <u>No Defaults</u>. No default (or breach which upon the expiration of any applicable grace period would constitute a default) exists under any insurance policy, lease, note, agreement, or other contractual obligation of or by which Seller is bound would have a material adverse affect on the business of or in the performance of this Agreement by the parties. In addition, no such breach will result in the acceleration of the maturity of or constitute a default under any insurance policy, lease, note, agreement, or other contractual obligation.

(i) <u>No Litigation</u>. There is no pending, contemplated or threatened litigation, action, suit, claim (including claims for unpaid taxes), proceeding, arbitration, or other procedure or governmental investigation against or affecting Seller, at law or in equity, before any court or tribunal or any federal, state, municipal or other governmental department, body, authority, commission, board, bureau, agency or-instrumentality, domestic or foreign, which would have a material or adverse affect on Seller or on its financial condition, on any of its businesses, assets, rights or properties or on the transactions contemplated herein. In addition, there are no unsatis-fied judgments, awards or decrees against Seller or against its businesses, properties or assets.

(j) <u>No Undisclosed Liabilities</u>. As of _____, 19___, Seller has no debt, liability or obligation of any nature, whether accrued, absolute, contingent or otherwise, and whether due or to become due, except as set forth or reserved against on its balance sheet dated _____, 19____.

(k) <u>Taxes</u>. Seller has filed all required federal, state, county and local income, excise, property and other tax returns. All taxes and/or assessments that have or may become due have been paid, including sales taxes imposed, and other duties or charges levied, assessed or imposed upon the business, assets, property, income or earnings of any kind or description of Seller, except income taxes owed and accruing during the taxable year which includes the Closing Date hereunder. There are no tax deficiencies existing, proposed or threatened against Seller.

(l) <u>Operation of Business</u>. Since _____, 19___, Seller has operated and will continue, from and after said date to and including the Closing Date, to operate its business and to serve its customers in its normal and customary manner. Seller shall safeguard and maintain confidential any and all confidential information, trade secrets, customer lists and the like. Between the period commencing of _____, 19___, up to and including the Closing Date, there have been and will be no material changes in the assets, business conditions, prospects, policies or methods of operation of Seller or waiver of any of its rights thereto other than changes in the ordinary course of business, which changes have not and will not adversely affect the business, assets, prospects, condition or operation of Seller.

All transactions involving or using the assets, customers, furniture, fixtures, equipment, inventory, customer and supplier lists, name, stationery and advertising materials of Seller have been and will be usual and customary in its ordinary course of business including but not limited to the following:

(1)Declaring any bonus or increasing the rate or form of compensation payable to any agent or employee.

(2)Disposing of any of its properties or assets or waiving any rights thereto, except in the ordinary course of its business;

(3)Incurring any indebtedness or liability except in the ordinary course of its business, or causing any adverse change to be made in its business affairs, fairs, financial or otherwise, or allowing any tax or other liability to be extended by waiver of any statute of limitation or otherwise;

(4)Causing any material adverse change in its financial condition, liabilities, assets, business' or prospects;

(5)Causing any destruction of, damage to or loss of any of its assets (whether or not covered by insurance) that materially and adversely affects its financial condition, assets, business or prospects;

(6)Amending or terminating any contract, agreement or license to which it is a party;

(7)Making or guaranteeing a loan to any person or entity;

(8)Mortgaging, pledging or otherwise encumbering any of its assets;

(9)Waiving or releasing any of its rights or claims;

(10)   Causing any other event or condition which has or might reasonably be expected to have a material and adverse affect on its financial condition, business, assets or prospects.

(m) Expenditures. From and after _____, 19__, Seller will make no material expenditures without the prior written consent of Buyer other than the reasonable and customary purchase of inventory items necessary to carry on the business of Seller in its normal course up to and through the Closing Date.

(n) <u>Compliance With Laws</u>. Seller has complied with and is currently complying, in all respects, and is not in violation of, any and all applicable laws, orders, rules and regulations promulgated by any federal, state, local, municipal or other governmental authority or any department, board, body or agency thereof, relating to the operation and conduct of its property, assets and business. including but not limited to bulk sales and bulk transfer laws under the Uniform Commercial Code. There are no existing or threatened violations of any such law, order, rule or regulation. Seller has not received any notice of violation of any applicable building or zoning regulations or orders, or of any other law, order, regulation or requirement relating to the operation of its business or affecting its assets. Seller is not in default with respect to any order, writ, injunction or decree of any court or federal, state, municipal or other governmental department, commission, board, bureau, agency, or instrumentality, domestic or foreign. No approvals, agreements, authorizations, permits or consents are necessary in connection with this Agreement and the consummation of the transactions contemplated herein.

(o) <u>No Removal of Assets</u>. Seller from and after _____, 19___, and up to and including the Closing Date, has not and will not remove or permit the removal of any furniture, fixtures, equipment, inventory, customer and supplier lists, stationery and advertising materials from its place of business or dispose or permit the disposal or permit its assets except in the ordinary course of the business.

(p) <u>Restrictions on Operations</u>. Seller is not a party to any agreement or restriction which may adversely affect its business, property, assets, operations or condition, financial or otherwise.

(q) <u>Insurance</u>. Seller has maintained and will continue to maintain in full force and effect fire, liability, and other forms of insurance in amounts and against the liabilities, claims, casualties and risks which are customary for its business.

(r) <u>Certificates or Other Instruments</u>. All statements contained in any certificate or other instrument delivered by or on behalf of Seller pursuant to this Agreement, or in connection with the transactions contemplated hereby, shall be deemed as covenants, representations and warranties by Seller hereunder.

(s) <u>Complete Representation/No Material Omissions</u>. Seller is not party to any contract or commitment nor is a guarantor, co-maker or surety with regard to any obligation other than those obligations specifically described in the Financial Statements. All material facts concerning the substance of this Agreement have been disclosed by Seller to Buyer. The Financial Statements and all information recited in this Agreement including the covenants, representations and warranties made or to be made by Seller in this Agreement, and any statement or certificate furnished or to be furnished to Buyer pursuant to this Agreement, or in connection with the transactions contemplated hereby, are true and accurate and do not or will not contain any untrue, false or misleading statement with respect to any material fact or omit any material fact to make said statements or certificates misleading. Seller is not involved in any undisclosed transactions, proceedings or investigations, including claims for unpaid taxes, which might (i) materially or adversely affect the assets and/or the rights and obligations which are the subject of the sale and/or transfer hereunder or (ii) hinder or prevent the transactions contemplated by this Agreement.

(t) <u>No Finders' Fee or Brokerage Commission</u>. Seller is not a party to or is obligated under any agreement for the payment of any finders fee or brokerage commission with regard to the sale contemplated hereunder.

(u) <u>Asset Condition and Repair</u>. All assets including without limitation furniture, fixtures, and equipment being sold hereby are in good operating condition and repair. All inventory of Seller and other items sold pursuant to this Agreement are in good salable condition and in conformity with all applicable laws, ordinances and regulations.

(v) <u>No Employment Contracts</u>. Seller is not a party to, bound by nor liable on any written or oral agreement of employment which will continue to exist after the Closing Date.

(w) <u>Employee Benefits</u>. Seller is not a party to, bound by, nor liable on any written or oral agreement providing remuneration or benefits, to or for employees or others which will continue to exist after the Closing Date.

(x) <u>Product Warranties</u>. Seller has not made or given any warranty or guarantee with respect to any of its products or services.

(y) <u>Insurance in Force</u>. Seller has and will maintain in full force and effect up to and including the date of delivery of possession of all assets sold hereunder, the existing fire, liability and extended coverage insurance on its business and assets in such amounts and against such liabilities, claims, casualties, and risks which are customary for its assets and businesses. If, after the Execution Date, any part of such property is destroyed or substantially damaged by fire or other casualty, Buyer shall have the option to (i) cancel this Agreement in its entirety by giving prior written notice of such cancellation to Seller or (ii) carry out this Agreement in its entirety by giving prior written notice to Seller of such intention. In the event Buyer elects to continue with the Agreement, Buyer shall be entitled to the proceeds of any insurance on any assets so damaged or destroyed by fire or other casualty. If no such insurance exists or if the insurance proceeds are insufficient, Buyer shall be entitled to deduct from the amount due at Closing the replacement purchase price of all such damaged or destroyed items.

(z) <u>Preservation of Assets</u>.   Seller shall exercise its best efforts to preserve the continuity of the business of Seller up to and including _____, 19___.

(aa) <u>Buyer to Collect and Remit Accounts Receivable of Seller</u>. The accounts receivable being purchased by Buyer hereunder include only the accounts receivable due from sales made on or before _____, 19___. After the Closing Date, Buyer shall exercise diligent efforts (but shall not be required to institute a suit or take any other extraordinary action) to collect the various accounts receivable due with respect to the business previously operated by Seller. Buyer shall at intervals convenient to Buyer, but not less frequently than once a month, remit to Seller such amounts as are collected with respect to sales made after said date less such amounts as are required to be paid by Buyer for sales or other taxes on such amounts so collected.

(bb) <u>Execution of Documents Prior to Closing</u>. Seller shall have executed prior to Closing all certificates, applications, authorizations, approvals, consents, permits and other documents as may be required under the laws of any state, including without limitation the states of _____.

7. <u>Covenants, Representations and Warranties of Buyer</u>. Buyer covenants, represents and warrants to Seller as follows:

(a) <u>Good Standing</u>. Buyer is a corporation incorporated under the laws of the State of _____.

(b) <u>Authority</u>. Buyer is authorized to execute this Agreement and has taken all necessary steps to consummate the transactions contemplated herein. A copy of the Board of Director Resolution of Buyer authorizing the purchase of the assets of Seller and the execution of this Agreement is attached hereto as Schedule "F".

8. <u>Survival of Warranties</u>. The covenants, representations and warranties set forth herein are made as of the Execution Date, said covenants, representations and warranties shall be deemed confirmed as of the Closing Date and all such covenants, representations and warranties shall survive the making of this Agreement and the Closing.

9. <u>Indemnification</u>. Seller will indemnify, save and hold Buyer harmless from and against any and all (i) claims, demands, causes of action, liabilities and losses of every kind and nature whatsoever, together with costs and expenses, relating to, resulting or arising from the business, debts or liabilities of Seller, including without limitation claims, liens, or liabilities arising out of or resulting from any failure on the part of Seller to comply with certain provisions of the "Uniform Commercial Code--Bulk Transfers", (ii) damage or deficiency resulting from any misrepresentation, breach of warranty, or nonfulfillment of any covenant, representation, warranty, or agreement on the part of Seller under this Agreement, or from any misrepresentation in or omission from this Agreement or any certificate or other instrument furnished or to be furnished to Buyer hereunder and (iii) actions, suits, proceedings, demands, assessments, judgments, costs and expenses incident to any of the foregoing. Seller shall reimburse Buyer, and its successors or assigns, on demand, for any payment made by Buyer or its successors or assigns, at any time after the Closing hereunder with respect to any liability or claim to which the foregoing indemnity relates.

10. <u>No Assumption of Liabilities by Buyer</u>.   Nothing in this Agreement or otherwise shall constitute any agreement on the part of Buyer to assume any liabilities of any nature of Seller including without limitation accounts payable. All liabilities of Seller as of the Closing Date shall be the sole and complete responsibility of Seller and Seller shall pay and discharge said liabilities forthwith. In addition to the foregoing, Seller shall satisfy Buyer that all of the suppliers of Seller including suppliers of inventory have been paid in full, and that all sales or similar taxes that have become due have been paid, or that payment shall be made on or before the Closing Date. Furthermore, Seller shall similarly remain responsible for and shall pay all vacation pay, severance pay, and/or termination benefits for the employees of Seller that Buyer has terminated.

11. <u>Access and Information</u>. From and after the Execution Date, Seller shall offer to Buyer and its representatives (including counsel, accountants and engineers of Buyer) at all reasonable times during normal business hours, full and complete access to the personnel, properties, projects, contracts, commitments, books, records and minute books of Seller. In addition, Seller shall furnish to such officers and representatives of Buyer such other information as Buyer may reasonably request. Furthermore, Seller shall authorize its independent accountants to permit Buyer's agents and employees to examine all records and working papers pertaining to the Financial Statements and the tax returns of Seller.

12. <u>Representations Survive Closing</u>.

The covenants, representations, warranties, guarantees and agreements of the parties and the respective obligations to be performed as set forth herein or in any instrument, certificate, opinion or other writing provided for in this Agreement are effective as of the Execution Date, shall be deemed joint and several, shall be deemed confirmed as of the Closing Date and shall survive the making of this Agreement, the Closing hereunder, and any investigation at any time made by or on behalf of Buyer.

13. <u>Contingencies--Conditions Precedent to the Obligation of Buyer to Close</u>. The duty and obligation of Buyer to perform under the terms of this Agreements and to consummate the transactions contemplated herein are subject to and expressly conditioned upon the occurrence of all of the following conditions or events unless expressly waived in writing by Buyer. Nonfulfillment of any of the following contingencies on or before the Closing Date shall, at the option of Buyer, terminate and void this Agreement and any and all amounts previously paid by Buyer to Seller shall be returned to Buyer forthwith.

(a) <u>Covenants, Representations and Warranties of Seller</u>. All of the covenants, representations and warranties made by Seller hereunder shall be true and correct in all respects and not breached by Seller in any respect as of the Closing Date;

(b) <u>Compliance With This Agreement by Seller</u>. Seller shall have performed and complied with all covenants, agreements and conditions required by this Agreement to be conformed or complied with by Seller prior to or at the Closing;

(c) <u>Partial Inventory by Buyer</u>. Buyer shall have made, on or before the Closing, a physical inventory of all of the real and personal property of the Business, the results of which shall be satisfactory to Buyer in Buyer's sole and absolute discretion;

(d) <u>Approval of Counsel of Buyer</u>. Counsel for Buyer shall have approved all actions, proceedings, instruments and documents required to carry out this Agreement or incidental thereto, and all other legal matters related to this Agreement which, in the opinion of Counsel for Buyer, require review;

(e) <u>No Damage or Destruction</u>. No properties, assets or business shall have suffered on or before the Closing Date any destruction or damage by fire, accident or other casualty or Act of God exceeding _____ Dollars ($_____) in value that is not covered by insurance.

(f) <u>Contingency-Officer's Certificate</u>. Seller shall have delivered to Buyer a certificate of its President, dated as of the Closing Date, certifying in such detail as may be reasonably requested by Buyer, the fulfillment of all conditions specified in this Agreement;

(g) <u>Contingencies--Opinion of Counsel</u>. Seller shall have delivered to Buyer an opinion of counsel, dated as of the Closing Date, that (i) the corporate existence, good standing, and authority of Seller to consummate the transactions contemplated by this Agreement are as represented herein; (ii) that Seller (except as otherwise stated by such counsel), does not know or have any reasonable grounds to know of any litigation, proceeding, or governmental investigation , pending or threatened, against or relating to Seller, its properties or business; (iii) that this Agreement and the transactions contemplated herein will not violate the Articles of Incorporation, Bylaws, or any agreements of Seller; and (iv) this Agreement and the transactions contemplated herein will not be in violation of any state or federal statutes;

14. <u>To Be Delivered at Closing</u>. Seller shall deliver to Buyer at the Closing:

1.   A Bill of Sale executed by Seller conveying to Buyer the furniture, fixtures, equipment, inventory, customer and supplier lists, stationery, advertising materials and supplies referred to herein. A copy of said Bill of Sale is attached hereto as Schedule "G" and incorporated herein by this reference;

2.   An assignment of the name of the Business. A copy of said assignment is attached hereto as Schedule "H" and incorporated herein by this reference;

3.   Any and all necessary agreements, authorizations, consents, approvals and permits to transfer the assets to Buyer hereunder;

4.   A properly prepared and certified corporate resolution as required in this Agreement;

5.   A detailed listing of accounts receivable duly assigned to Buyer showing amounts due with respect to sales by Seller up to the Closing;

6.   A written representation from Seller that none of the covenants, representations and warranties of Seller contained herein have been breached in any respect as of the Closing Date. A copy of said representation is attached hereto as Schedule "I" and incorporated herein by this reference;

7.   The opinion of Seller's counsel in form and substance satisfactory to Buyer and its counsel that the covenants, representations and warranties hereof are absolutely true and correct.

8.   Such other instruments as may be necessary or incidental to carry out the intentions of the parties.

Buyer shall deliver to Seller at the Closing:

1.   Cash or a cashier's check, made payable to Seller in the amount of _____ Dollars ($_____) less any adjustments;

2.   A duly executed promissory note;

3.   A duly executed Security Agreement securing said promissory note;

4.   A duly executed trust deed on real estate located at _____ securing said promissory note.

5.   A current Certificate of Good Standing for Buyer issued by the Secretary of State of _____ ;

6.   A Certified Board of Directors Resolution from Buyer authorizing the purchase of the assets of Seller; and

7.   Such other instruments as may be necessary or incidental to carry out the intentions of the parties.

15. <u>Indemnification</u>. <u>Seller Indemnifies Buyer - Seller Retains Right to Defend.</u>   Seller indemnifies, defends, protects, saves and holds Buyer harmless at all times after the Execution Date from and against any and all liabilities, losses, damages, claims, costs, recoveries, deficiencies, actions, causes of action, suits, liens, proceedings, demands, assessments, judgments of every kind or nature whatsoever, together with costs and expenses, including interest, penalties, court costs and reasonable attorneys' fees, occasioned by, relating to, resulting from or arising out of any breach, default or failure to perform by Seller or its employees or agents of any representation, warranty, covenant or promise contained herein or from any act, misrepresentation or omission to act by Seller or its employees or agents including but not limited to:

(a)   The business, debts or liabilities of Seller;

(b)   Claims, liens, or liabilities arising out of or resulting from any failure on the part of Seller to comply with the provisions of the "Uniform Commercial Code--Bulk Transfers";

(c)   Any damage or deficiency resulting from any misrepresentation, breach or nonfulfillment of any covenant, representation, warranty or agreement on the part of Seller pursuant to this Agreement; and

(d)   Any misrepresentation in or omission from this Agreement or any certificate or other instrument furnished or to be furnished to Buyer hereunder.

Seller shall immediately reimburse Buyer on demand for any payment made by Buyer or its successors or assigns at any time on or after the Closing with respect to any liability or claim to which the foregoing indemnity relates.

In the event Buyer learns of a claim against Buyer which, if allowed (either by voluntary payment, settlement or compromise or by a court of law or equity, or by other judicial or quasi-judicial tribunals or agencies) would result in damages payable by Seller hereunder, before payment or agreeing to pay the same, Buyer shall promptly notify Seller in writing of all such facts within Buyer's knowledge with respect to such claims and the amounts thereof. If, prior to the expiration of thirty (30) days from the date of mailing of said notice, Seller shall state in writing that such claim shall not be paid, Buyer shall refrain from paying the same, and Seller shall on Seller's own behalf in good faith at its own expense undertake the handling, defense, settlement, compromise or litigation of said claim.

The right of Seller to undertake the defense of any such claim shall be conditioned on Seller posting for the benefit of Buyer within said thirty (30) day period an indemnity bond or other security satisfactory to Buyer in an amount equal to the amount in controversy. In lieu of posting a bond, reasonable arrangements acceptable to both parties for the deposit of funds or property into escrow (including the promissory note from Buyer to Seller) may be made. Buyer shall cooperate fully in attempting to defend or minimize the liability of Seller hereunder. Notwithstanding the foregoing, in the event that any claim shall have been adjudicated by a court of competent jurisdiction, and a judgment or decree has been entered (unless an appeal is taken therefrom and a proper appeal bond posted by Seller), Buyer may pay any such matured claim or any other claim at any time where the failure to make such payment would result in the foreclosure of a lien upon any property then held by Buyer.

In the event Seller fails to give such notice to Buyer, or fails to undertake the settlement, compromise, or litigation with respect to such claim, Buyer shall be authorized to undertake the defense, compromise, settlement and payment of such claim on behalf of and as agent for Seller, and shall be fully entitled to indemnification therefor by Seller pursuant to this Agreement.

16. <u>Expenses</u>. Each of the parties hereto shall pay his or its own costs and expenses, including legal fees, incurred or to be incurred in the drafting and negotiating of this Agreement and the carrying out the transactions contemplated herein. Notwithstanding the foregoing, in the event of a breach of this Agreement by either Buyer or Seller, all costs and expenses, including legal fees, incurred by Buyer shall be immediately reimbursed by Seller.

_____
Seller

_____
Buyer

SAMPLE

STOCK SALE AGREEMENT

This Agreement of Purchase and Sale of Stock ("Agreement") is made and entered into as of _____, 19___ by and between _____ ("Buyer") and _____ (the "Shareholders").

<u>RECITALS</u>

A.

B.

C.

<u>AGREEMENT</u>

IN CONSIDERATION of the provisions and agreements herein contained, the parties agree as follows:

1. <u>Purchase and Sale of Shares</u>.

Subject to the terms and conditions set forth in this Agreement, on the Closing Date (as hereinafter defined), the Shareholders will transfer and convey _____ shares of common stock (the "Shares") to Buyer, and Buyer will acquire the Shares from the Shareholders.

2.   Purchase Price and Payment of Purchase Price.

2.1 Purchase Price. As full consideration for the sale of the Shares to Buyer, Buyer shall pay to the Shareholders, in the manner prescribed in Section 2.2 below, the sum of _____ Dollars ($_____) (the "Purchase Price").

2.2 Payment of the Purchase Price. The Purchase Price shall be paid as follows:

(a) Buyer shall pay to the Shareholders on the Closing Date, by certified or cashier's check, the sum of _____ Dollars ($_____); and

(b) Buyer shall deliver to the Shareholders on the Closing Date a promissory note (the "Note") in the principal amount of _____. The Note shall be in the form of Exhibit "A" attached hereto and incorporated herein by this reference.

3.   Representations and Warranties of Shareholders.

The Shareholders jointly and severally make the following representations and warranties (except as disclosed in a disclosure schedule delivered concurrently herewith in which all exceptions are noted by specific reference to the Section for which the exception is being made (the "Disclosure Schedule"):

3.1 Authority. This Agreement has been only authorized, executed and delivered by each of the Shareholders, and no further action, approvals or consents are necessary on the part of any of the Shareholders or any other party, including governmental agencies, to take this Agreement valid and binding upon the Shareholders in accordance with its terms, or to enable the Shareholders to perform this Agreement and the transactions contemplated thereby.

3.2<u>Organization and Good Standing</u>. The Corporation is a corporation duly organized, validly existing and in good standing under the laws of the State of _____. It is not required to qualify to do business in any other jurisdiction as a result of the nature of its business or the character or location of its properties, or otherwise, other than jurisdictions in which the failure to so qualify would not have a material adverse effect on it. The Corporation has full power to carry on its business as it is now, and since its organization has been, conducted, and is entitled to own, lease and/or operate its properties and assets which it now owns, leases or operates. The Corporation: will within a reasonable time prior to the Closing Date furnish to Buyer for examination has delivered to Buyer true and correct copies of (i) its Articles of Incorporation and all amendments thereto, (ii) its Bylaws (duly certified by its corporate secretary) and all amendments thereto, and minute and stock books, and (iii) any agreements among any of its Shareholders. The Corporation has complied and is currently in compliance with all federal, state and local laws, regulations and orders applicable to its business, except as disclosed in the Disclosure Schedule.

3.3   <u>Subsidiaries</u>. The Corporation does not own or control directly or indirectly any interest or investment (whether equity or debt) in any joint venture, corporation, partnership, proprietorship, or other entity.

3.4   <u>Capitalization</u>. The authorized capital stock of the Corporation, the number of issued and outstanding shares and the record and beneficial owners thereof are all set forth on Exhibit "B" attached hereto and incorporated herein by this reference. All of the issued and outstanding shares of the Corporation are validly issued and outstanding, fully paid and nonassessable, and are not issued in violation of any preemptive rights of any stockholder or in violation or contravention of any agreement to which any of the Shareholders or the Corporation are a party. Neither the Corporation nor any of the Shareholders have granted, or is a party to any agreements, commitments or understandings providing for the grant of, subscriptions, options, or other rights to purchase or receive, or obligating any of the Shareholders or the Corporation to issue, sell or otherwise transfer, any shares of capital stock of any class of the Corporation or any options or warrants to purchase, or any securities convertible into, shares of any class of capital stock of the Corporation.

3.5 <u>Title to Shares</u>. The Shareholders own, beneficially and of record, the Shares set forth opposite their respective names on Exhibit "C" attached hereto and incorporated herein by this reference. All of the Shares are and on the Closing Date will be free and clear of all liens, encumbrances, security agreements, equities, options, claims, charges, and restrictions other than the restriction on transferability imposed by the California Commissioner of Corporations which is set forth on the share certificates. The Shares now and on the Closing Date will constitute one hundred percent (100%) of the issued and outstanding equity securities of the Corporation. The Shareholders have full power to transfer the Shares to Buyer without obtaining the consent or approval of any other person or governmental authority other than the consent of the California Commissioner of Corporations.

3.6 <u>Financial Statements</u>. The Shareholders have delivered to Buyer the balance sheet(s) of the Corporation for the fiscal year(s) ended 19___ , together with related statements of income, retained earnings, and changes in financial position for the ___ year(s) period ending on such/those/date(s), audited by _____, certified public accountants, whose reports thereon are included therewith, and unaudited balance sheet(s) as of 19__, together with related unaudited statements of income and retained earnings, and changes in financial condition, for the _____ month period ended _____, certified by the Corporation's President and Chief Financial

Officer. All of the foregoing are collectively referred to as the "Financial Statements". The Financial Statements (i) were prepared in accordance with generally accepted accounting principles consistently applied throughout the periods indicated; and (ii) fairly present the Corporation's financial condition and the results of operations as of the relevant dates thereof and for the periods covered thereby.

3.7   Absence of Undisclosed Liabilities.   The Corporation has no debt, liability, or obligation of any nature, whether accrued, absolute, contingent, or otherwise, and whether due or to become due, that is not reflected or reserved against in the Corporation's balance sheet as of 19__, included in the Financial Statements or set forth in the Disclosure Schedule, except for those (i) that may have been incurred after the date of that balance sheet and (ii) that are not required by generally accepted accounting principles to be included in a balance sheet. All debts, liabilities, and obligations incurred after that date were incurred in the ordinary course of business, and are usual and normal in amount both individually and in the aggregate.

3.8   Absence of Specified Changes.   Since _____, 19__ there has not been any:

(i)   Transaction by the Corporation except in the ordinary course of business as conducted on that date;

(ii)   Capital expenditures by the Corporation exceeding $_____;

(iii)   Material or adverse change in the financial condition, liabilities, assets, business, or prospects of the Corporation;

(iv) Destruction, damage to, or loss of any asset of the Corporation (whether or not covered by insurance) that materially and adversely affects the financial condition, business, or prospects of the Corporation;

(v) Labor trouble or other event or condition of any character materially and adversely affecting the financial condition, business, assets, or prospects of the Corporation;

(vi) Change in accounting methods or practices (including, without limitation, any change in depreciation or amortization policies or rates) by the Corporation;

(vii) Revaluation by the Corporation of any of its assets;

(viii) Declaration, setting aside, or payment of a dividend or other distribution in respect to the capital stock of the Corporation, or any direct or indirect redemption, purchase, or other acquisition by the Corporation of any of its shares of capital stock;

(ix) Increase in the salary or other compensation payable or to become payable by the Corporation, to any of its officers, directors, agents, or independent contractors, or the declaration, payment, commitment or obligation of any kind for the payment, by the Corporation, of a bonus or other additional salary or compensation to any such person except to employees who are not officers, in the ordinary course of business;

(x) Sale or transfer of any asset or cancellation of or claim of the Corporation, except in the ordinary course of business;

(xi) Amendment or termination of any contract, agreement, or license to which the Corporation is a party except in the ordinary course of business;

(xii) Loan by the Corporation to any person or entity;

(xiii) Mortgage, pledge, or other encumbrance of any asset of the Corporation, except liens for taxes not yet due;

(xiv) Waiver or release of any right or claim of the Corporation, except in the ordinary course of business;

(xv) Other event or condition of any character that has or might reasonably have a material and adverse effect on the financial condition, business, assets, or prospects of the Corporation;

(xvi) Issuance or sale by the Corporation of any shares of its capital stock of any class, or of any other of its securities; or

(xvii) Any commitment by the Corporation to issue any shares of its capital stock or other equity securities, or any options, rights to purchase, or securities convertible into any capital stock or other equity securities of the Corporation;

(xviii) Indebtedness incurred for borrowed money or any commitment to borrow money, or any guaranty or commitment to guaranty the indebtedness of others entered into by the Corporation;

(xix) Any other event or condition of any character which has a material and adverse effect on the properties, business or prospects of the Corporation;

(xx) Agreement by the Corporation to do any of the things described in the preceding clauses (i) through (xix);

3.9 <u>Real and Tangible Personal Property</u>. Exhibit "I" attached hereto and incorporated herein by this reference is a list of all real property owned or leased by the Corporation, which list includes (i) the address of each such real property, and (ii) whether the real property is owned or leased from others by the Corporation. Exhibit "J" attached hereto and incorporated herein by this reference is a complete and accurate list describing, and specifically the location of, all tangible personal property owned or leased by the Corporation (except inventory items), including all such property included in the balance sheet under the heading "Property, Plant and Equipment." Exhibit "K" attached hereto and incorporated herein by this reference is a list of the real and personal property leases, respectively, to which the Corporation is a party (the "Real Property Leases" and "Personal Property Leases", respectively). The Shareholders have delivered to Buyer (i) a description of all the real properties owned or leased by the Corporation, and the buildings, fixtures and other improvements thereon, (ii) true and correct copies of preliminary title reports (dated not earlier than 10 days prior to delivery) with respect to each of the real properties listed in Exhibit "I" (the "Title Reports"), together with true and correct copies of all exceptions shown thereon, and (iii) true and correct copies of all of the Real Property Leases and the Personal Property Leases. All personal property used in the Corporation's operations is owned by the Corporation, except for any personal property, the subject of any of the Personal Property Leases, and no such personal property has been removed. All of the real and personal property reflected on Exhibits "I" and "J", or the subject of the Real and Personal Property

Leases, constitute all of the real and personal property necessary for the conduct by the Corporation of its business as now conducted, and is in good condition and repair, ordinary wear and tear excepted. Except as provided in the Real Property Leases and the Personal Property Leases, no real or personal property used by the Corporation in connection with its business is held under any lease, security agreement, conditional sales contract, or other title retention or security arrangement, or is other than in the exclusive possession and control of the Corporation.

3.10   Inventory.   The inventories of raw materials, work in process and finished goods (collectively "inventories") of the Corporation on the Closing Date will (i) consist of items of a quality and quantity usable and saleable in the ordinary course of business and, (ii) in any event, not be of a quantity in excess of what can be sold in the ordinary course of business during the twelve months immediately following the Closing Date. All items included in the inventories are the property of the Corporation, except for sales made in the ordinary course of business since _____. For each of these sales either the purchaser has made full payment or the purchaser's liability to make payment is reflected on the books of the Corporation. No items included in the inventories have been pledged as collateral or are held by the Corporation on consignment from others.

3.11   Accounts Receivables.   The accounts receivable reflected in the _____ balance sheets (included in the Financial Statements) and all accounts receivable created after _____, arose from valid sales in the ordinary course of business and have been collected or are collectible in full.

3.12   Patents and Patent Rights.   Exhibit "L" attached hereto and incorporated herein by this reference is a complete schedule of all patents, inventions, industrial models, processes, designs and applications for patents owned by the Corporation or in which it has any rights, licenses or communities. The patents and patent applications for patents listed on Exhibit "L" are valid and in full force and effect and are not subject to any taxes, maintenance fees or actions. There have not been any interference actions or other judicial, arbitration or other adversary proceedings concerning these patents or applications for patents. The manufacture, use or sale of the inventions, models, designs and systems covered by these patents and applications for patents do not violate or infringe on any patent or any proprietary or personal right of any person, firm or corporation; and the Corporation has not infringed nor is now infringing on any patent or other right belonging to any person, firm or corporation. The Corporation is not a party to any license, agreement or arrangement, whether as licensee, licensor or otherwise, with respect to any patent, application for patent, invention, design, model, process, trade secret or formula. The Corporation has the right and authority to use such inventions, trade secrets, processes, models, designs and formulas as are necessary to enable it to conduct and to continue to conduct all phases of its business in the manner presently conducted by it, and that use does not, and will not, conflict with, infringe on, or violate any patent or other rights of others.

3.13 Copyrights, Trade Names and Trademarks. Exhibit "M" attached hereto and incorporated herein by this reference is a schedule of all trade names, trademarks, service marks, and copyrights and their registrations owned by the Corporation or in which it has any rights or licenses, together with a brief description of each. The Corporation has not infringed, and is not now infringing, on any trade name, trademark, service mark, or copyright belonging to any other person, firm, or corporation. The Corporation is not a party to any license, agreement, or arrangement, whether as licensor, licensee, or otherwise, with respect to any trademarks, service marks, trade names, or applications for them, or any copyrights. The Corporation owns, or holds adequate licenses or other rights to use, all trademarks, service marks, trade names, and copyrights necessary for its business as now conducted by it and that use does not, and will not, conflict with, infringe on, or otherwise violate any rights of others. Exhibit "M" also contains a complete and accurate list of all intangibles, other than specifically referred to elsewhere in this Agreement, and the nature and location of certificates or other evidences of the Corporation's title thereto.

     3.14   <u>Trade Secrets</u>. Exhibit "N" attached hereto and incorporated herein by this reference is a true and complete list, without extensive or revealing descriptions, of the Corporation's trade secrets, including all secret formulas, customer lists, processes, know-how, computer programs and other technical data. The specific location of each trade secret's documentation, including its complete description, specifications, charts, procedures, and other material relating to it, also set forth with it in that exhibit. Each trade secret's documentation is current, accurate, and sufficient in detail and content to identify and explain it, and to allow its full and proper use by Buyer without reliance on the special knowledge or memory of others.

     The Corporation is the sole owner of each of these trade secrets, free and clear of any liens, encumbrances, restrictions, or legal or equitable claims of others. The Corporation has taken all reasonable security measures to protect the secrecy, confidentiality, and value of these trade secrets; any of its employees and other persons who, either alone or in concert with others, developed, invented, discovered, derived, programmed, or designed these secrets, or who have knowledge of or access to information relating to them, have been put on notice and, if appropriate, have entered into agreements that these secrets are proprietary to the Corporation and not to be divulged or misused.

All of these trade secrets are presently valid and protectable, and are not part of the public knowledge or literature, nor to Shareholders' knowledge have they been used, divulged, or appropriated for the benefit of any past or present employees or other persons, or to the detriment of the Corporation.

3.15 <u>Title and Quite Enjoyment</u>. The Corporation has good and marketable title of its assets and interests in assets, whether real, personal, mixed, tangible, and intangible, which constitute all the assets and interests in assets that are used in its business, including, without limitation, the assets reflected in the balance sheet included in the Financial Statements, assets acquired thereafter, and the assets described as being owned by the Corporation pursuant to this Section 3.15. All of these assets are free and clear of restrictions on or conditions to transfer or assignment, and are free and clear of mortgages, liens, pledges, charges, encumbrances, equities, claims, easements, rights of way, covenants, conditions, or restrictions, except for (i) those disclosed in Financial Statements, or in the Title Reports; (ii) the lien of current taxes not yet due and payable; (iii) those disclosed in the Disclosure Schedule; (iv) those disclosed in any of the Real or Personal Property Leases; and (v) possible minor matters that, in the aggregate, are not substantial in amount and do not detract from or interfere with the present or intended use of any of these assets, nor impair business operations of the Corporation. The zoning of each parcel of real property owned, or leased from others, by the Corporation permits the presently existing improvements and the continuation of the business presently conducted thereon. The Corporation is in possession of all properties leased to it from others. The Corporation will continue to be entitled, following the consummation of the transactions contemplated hereby, to quite enjoyment and use of all real and personal properties and assets currently leased by it from others without disturbance whether due to any default by the Corporation or the consummation of the transactions contemplated hereby or otherwise.

3.16 <u>Leases</u>. The Real and Personal Property Leases (the "Leases") are valid and binding obligations of the parties thereto in accordance with their respective terms, and are now and on the Closing Date will be in full force and effect. As of the Closing Date, no party to any such Lease will be in default with respect to any term or condition thereof, nor will there be any event that has occurred or is expected to occur which, with the passage of time or the giving of notice, or both, would constitute a default thereunder, or would cause the acceleration of any obligations of any party thereto or the creation of a lien or encumbrance upon any properties or assets of the Corporation. None of the Leases contain any provisions which, after the Closing Date, would (i) hinder or prevent the Corporation from continuing to use any of the properties or assets in the manner in which they are currently used or (ii) impose any additional costs (other than scheduled rental increases) or burdensome requirements as a condition to their continued use which are not currently in effect. The Corporation shall not modify or amend or agree to modify or amend any of the Leases between the date hereof and the Closing Date. The Shareholders shall deliver to Buyer on the Closing Date (i) estoppel certificates from each of the lessors under the Leases (dated not more than _____ days prior to the Closing Date, confirming that the Leases are in full force and effect, that there have been no defaults thereunder and that there are no events which have occurred or are anticipated to occur which, with the passage of time or the giving of notice, or both, would constitute a default under any of the Leases, and (ii) all consents which are required under any of the Leases in connection with this Agreement and the consummation of the transactions contemplated hereby.

3.17 <u>Condition of Properties</u>. All tangible properties and assets, real, personal and mixed, of the Corporation are in good working condition, normal and reasonable wear and tear excepted.

3.18   <u>Contracts and Agreements</u>. The Shareholders have delivered to Buyer true and correct copies of all contracts, agreements, arrangements and commitments with respect to or affecting the conduct of the business of the Corporation. Each of such contracts, agreements, arrangements and commitments is a valid and binding obligation of the parties thereto in accordance with its terms and there have been no defaults or claims of default and there are no facts or conditions that have occurred or that are anticipated to occur which, through the passage of time or the giving of notice, or both, would constitute a default thereunder or would cause the acceleration of any obligation of any party thereto or the creation of a lien or encumbrance upon any asset of the Corporation. Neither the execution and delivery of this Agreement not the consummation of the transactions contemplated hereby will require the consent of any party to any of such contracts, agreements, arrangements or commitments.

3.19   <u>Labor and Employment Agreements</u>. Neither, the Corporation nor its business has any (i) collective bargaining agreement or other labor agreement to which it is a party, or by which it is bound; (ii) employment, profit sharing, deferred compensation, bonus, pension, retainer, consulting, retirement, welfare or incentive plan or contract to which it is a party, or by which it is bound; (iii) written or other formal personnel policies; or (iv) plan or agreement under which "fringe benefits" (including, but not limited to, vacation plans or programs, sick leave plans or programs, and related benefits) are afforded to its employees. True and correct copies of all of the foregoing items, if any, set forth or referenced in the Disclosure Schedule have been delivered to Buyer.

3.20   <u>Agreement Will Not Cause Breach</u>. Neither the execution and delivery of, nor the consummation of the transactions contemplated by, this Agreement will result in or constitute any of the following: (i) a default or an event that, with notice or lapse of time, or both, would be a default, breach or violation of the Articles of Incorporation or Bylaws of the Corporation or any lease, license, franchise, promissory note, conditional sales contract, commitment, indenture, mortgage, deed of trust, or other agreement, instrument or arrangement to which any of the Shareholders or the Corporation is a party or by which any of them or the property of any of them is bound; (ii) an event that would permit any person to terminate any agreement or to accelerate the maturity of any indebtedness or other obligation of any of the Shareholders or the Corporation; (iii) the creation or imposition of any lien, charge or encumbrance on any of the properties of any of the Shareholders or the Corporation; (iv) a violation or breach of any writ, injunction or decree of any court or governmental instrumentality to which any of the Shareholders or the Corporation is a party or by which it or any of their properties are bound; or (v) a loss or adverse modification of any license, franchise or other authorization granted to or otherwise held by any of the Shareholders or the Corporation.

3.21 Insurance Coverage. The Shareholders have delivered to Buyer a copy of each insurance policy maintained by the Corporation with respect to the businesses and properties of the Corporation, or, if self-insured, a copy of all pertinent certificates, bonds, plans and other data relating to such self-insurance program. All the insurable properties and operations of the Corporation are insured for their respective benefit in adequate amounts against customary risks of physical damage. Such insurance policies have been in force and effect continuously, without gaps in coverage, for at least the past _____ years, and will be outstanding and in full force and effect on and at the Closing Date. In addition, the Corporation has been continuously covered, without gaps in such coverage, by general public liability and worker's compensation (or approved self-insurance programs in the case of worker's compensation) during the past _____ year period. Exhibit "O" attached hereto and incorporated herein by this reference contains a list of the names of each property, casualty and liability insurance carrier which maintains as of the date hereof a policy covering a risk of the Corporation, together with a statement of the nature of such insurance, the policy limits and the annual premium. The Shareholders have also delivered to Buyer a statement by the Corporation's insurer or agent stating that there have been no known, undisclosed gaps in such coverage for the periods of time addressed herein. The Shareholders specifically warrant that there have been no gaps in the Corporation's worker's compensation and general public liability insurance for the past _____ years, that all such insurance was and is adequate, and that all such insurance will be outstanding and in full force and effect on the Closing Date.

3.22 <u>Taxes and Tax Returns</u>. Within the times and in the manner prescribed by law, including extensions, the Corporation has filed and will continue to file up through the Closing Date all federal, state, local and other governmental (both domestic and foreign) tax returns and similar reports required to be filed by it, and has paid and will continue to pay up through the Closing Date all taxes shown thereon which are due and payable including, without limitation, income tax. All taxes, assessments and levies which the Corporation is required by law to withhold, collect or pay, including, without limitation, federal and state employee income tax withholding, have been withheld or collected and paid over to the proper governmental authorities. Up through the Closing Date, the Corporation will continue to withhold or collect, and pay such taxes, assessments and levies to the proper governmental authorities. The provisions for taxes reflected in the Corporation's balance sheet as of _____, are adequate for any and all federal, state, county, local and foreign taxes for the period ending on such date and for all prior periods, whether or not disputed. There are not present disputes as to taxes of any nature payable by the Corporation nor does the Corporation have any reasonable grounds to anticipate any audit of any of its tax returns. The Shareholders have delivered to Buyer true and complete copies of the Federal and State income tax returns filed by the Corporation for its fiscal years ending _____. The Shareholders have also delivered to Buyer complete copies of the sales, use and personal property tax returns filed by the Corporation for its fiscal years ending _____.

3.23   Compliance With Law. The Shareholders have delivered to Buyer a list of all licenses, permits and certificates obtained for the business of the Corporation. Except as disclosed in the Disclosure Schedule, (i) the operations of the Corporation have not been and are not now in violation of any federal, state or local laws, regulations or orders (including, without limitation applicable building and zoning laws, ordinances or regulations) which have or will have a material and adverse effect on the business of the Corporation; and (ii) the Corporation has all licenses, permits, and certificates from governmental agencies necessary for the conduct of its business as now conducted. No claim has been made by any governmental authority (and no such claim is anticipated by the Corporation) to the effect that the business conducted by the Corporation fails to comply, in any respect, with any law, rule, regulation or ordinance or that a license, permit or order is necessary with respect thereto (without such license, permit or order having been obtained promptly after the receipt of notice of such claim).

3.24   Litigation and Proceedings.   There are no actions, suits or proceedings (whether or not purportedly on behalf of the Corporation) pending or, to the knowledge of the Corporation or the Shareholders, threatened against or affecting the Corporation, at law or in equity, or before or by any governmental department, commission, board, bureau, agency or instrumentality, domestic or foreign, or before any arbitrator of any kind, which involve the possibility of any judgment or liability, or which may become a claim against Buyer or the Corporation. The Corporation is not subject to or in default under any judgment, order, writ, injunction, decree, or award of any court, arbitrator or governmental department, commission, board, bureau, agency or instrumentality.

3.25   Adverse Agreements. The Corporation is not a party to any agreement or instrument or subject to any charter or other corporate restriction, which adversely affects or in the future could adversely affect the Corporation's properties, assets, conditions or prospects.

3.26   Brokerage and Finder's Fees. The Shareholders nor the Corporation has incurred any unpaid liability to any broker, finder or agent for any brokerage fees, finder's fees or commissions with respect to the transactions contemplated by this Agreement, and the Shareholders shall indemnify and hold harmless Buyer from and against any and all such fees and commissions.

3.27   Labor Disputes. There is not now pending or threatened, nor during the past _____ years have there been threatened, any labor dispute, strike or work stoppage which affects, or may affect, or did or could have affected the business of the Corporation, or which may disrupt or could have disrupted its operations.

3.28   Adverse Facts and Circumstances. Neither the Shareholders nor the Corporation know of any facts or circumstances which might result in any adverse change in the condition, financial or otherwise, business or prospects of the Corporation or which might adversely affect its properties or assets.

3.29   Certain Transactions. The Corporation is not indebted, either directly or indirectly, to any of its shareholders, officers, directors, or any entity in which any of them have an interest ("Affiliates"), in any amount whatsoever; nor are any of its shareholders, officers, directors, or Affiliates indebted to the Corporation; nor are there are transactions of a continuing nature between the Corporation and any of its shareholders, officers, directors or Affiliates (other than by or through the regular employment thereof by the Corporation) not subject to cancellation, which will continue beyond the Closing Date, including, without limitation, use of the Corporation's assets for personal benefit with or without adequate compensation, or similar transactions; and all related-party indebtedness to the Corporation by any Shareholder, officer, director or Affiliate will be satisfied on or before the Closing Date.

3.30   Customers and Vendors. The Shareholders have delivered to Buyer a true and correct list of (i) the names of each customer who has purchased more than $_____ of goods from the Corporation in any of the last _____ calendar years and the amounts so purchased, and (ii) the names of each vendor from whom the Corporation has purchased more than $_____ of goods in any of the last _____ calendar years and the amounts so purchased. Neither the Corporation nor the Shareholders are aware of any facts indicating that any of the foregoing customers or vendors intend to cease doing business with the Corporation or materially after the amount of business they are presently doing with the Corporation.

3.31   Salaries.   Exhibit "P" attached hereto and incorporated herein by this reference sets forth the names, current annual salary and terms of employment (including the terms of any contract, profit sharing, bonus or other form of compensation other than salary paid or payable) to each officer, director and other employee of the Corporation whose current annual salary is in excess of $_____ or who has a contract of employment with the Corporation that cannot be terminated without cause and without liability upon 30 days notice or less. No salaries or benefits owed to any employee are in arrears.

3.32   <u>Bank Accounts</u>. Exhibit 3.32 lists the name and location of each bank or other institution in which the Corporation has a bank account, instrument of deposit or safe deposit box, and the names of all persons authorized to draw thereon or who have access thereto.

3.33   <u>Interest in Customers, Suppliers and Competitors</u>. Except as disclosed in the Disclosure Schedule and, except for minor stock interests (defined as less than one percent (1%)) in publicly traded companies, no officer, employee, Shareholder or director of the Corporation, nor any spouse, child or relative of any of them (i) has an interest, direct or indirect, as a shareholder, partner, officer, director, employee, creditor or otherwise in any firm, corporation or other entity which is engaged in any activity substantially competitive with the activities of the Corporation, or which is a supplier, distributor, customer or landlord of the Corporation, or (ii) owns, directly or indirectly, in whole or in part, any patents, trademarks, trade names, copyrights or applications therefor or any license under any thereof which the Corporation is using or the use of which is necessary for its business as now conducted.

3.34   <u>Employee Benefit Payments</u>. As of _____ the Corporation has, for all employee benefits, filed all statements and forms and paid or remitted all payments due, including but not limited to FICA, workmens' compensation, employee insurance and state disability insurance, and unemployment compensation contributions and will continue to make all such filings and payments through the Closing Date.

3.35   <u>Corporate Actions</u>. All corporate actions required of the Corporation in the proper conduct of its business have been taken, and all reports and returns required to be filed have been filed. The books and records of the Corporation, including, without limitation, the books of account, minute books, stock certificate books and stock ledger are complete and correct in all material respects and fairly reflect the conduct of the business of the Corporation.

    3.36   <u>Powers of Attorney</u>. Exhibit "R" attached hereto and incorporated herein by this reference is a list of all persons holding powers of attorney from the Corporation and a summary of the terms thereof.

    3.37   <u>Material Misstatements or Omissions</u>. No representations or warranties of any of the Shareholders contained in this Agreement or in any document, statement or certificate furnished or to be furnished pursuant hereto, or in connection with the transactions contemplated hereby, contain or on the Closing Date will contain an untrue statement of a material fact, or omit or on the Closing Date will omit to state a material fact necessary to make the statements of facts therein not misleading.

    4.   <u>Representations and Warranties of Buyer</u>.

    Buyer makes the following representations and warranties:

    4.1 <u>Organization and Good Standing</u>. Buyer is a corporation duly organized, existing and in good standing under the laws of _____.

    4.2 <u>Authority</u>. The execution and delivery of this Agreement and the consummation of this transaction by Buyer have been duly authorized, and no further corporate authorization is necessary on the part of Buyer.

    4.3 <u>Brokerage and Finder's Fees</u>. Buyer has not incurred any unpaid liability to any broker, finder or agent for any brokerage fees, finder's fees or commissions with respect to the transactions contemplated by this Agreement, and Buyer shall indemnify and hold harmless the Shareholders from and against any and all such fees and commissions [including fees and commissions to _____.

4.4 <u>Investment Representation</u>. Buyer represents that the Shares are to be received by it for investment and not for distribution, acknowledges that the Shares have not been registered with the Securities and Exchange Commission ("SEC") or qualified with the California Department of Corporations and acknowledges that the Shares cannot be sold or otherwise transferred without such registration with the SEC and qualification under the state securities laws of the state of such sale or transfer, or pursuant to an exemption from such registration or qualification.

5.   <u>Shareholders' Obligations Before Closing</u>.

The Shareholders agree that between the date hereof and the Closing Date:

5.1 <u>Corporate Matters</u>. The Corporation will not (i) amend its Articles of Incorporation or Bylaws; (ii) issue any shares of capital stock; (iii) issue or create any warrants, obligations, subscriptions, options, convertible securities or other commitments under which any additional shares of its capital stock of any class might be directly or indirectly authorized, issued, or transferred; or (iv) agree to do any of the above.

5.2 <u>Access and Information</u>. The Corporation will afford to Buyer and its counsel, accountants and other representatives full access during normal business hours throughout the period prior to the Closing Date to all the properties, books, contracts, records, and documents of or relating to the Corporation, and will furnish them with all the information, including copies of books, records and contracts, which they may reasonably request.

5.3 <u>Conduct of Business</u>. The Corporation will conduct its business diligently and in substantially the same manner as it previously has been carried out, and the Corporation shall not make or institute any unusual or novel methods of manufacture, purchase, sale, lease, management, accounting, or operation that will vary materially from those methods used by the Corporation as of the date of this Agreement. All of the Corporation's assets shall be maintained in the same condition as on the date hereof, ordinary wear and tear excepted.

5.4 <u>Preservation of Business and Relationships</u>. The Shareholders will use their best efforts to preserve the Corporation's business organization, to keep available to the Corporation its present officers and employees, and to preserve the Corporation's present relationships with suppliers, customers, and others having business relationships with it.

5.5 <u>Employees and Compensation</u>. The Corporation will not do, or agree to do, any of the following acts:

    (a) Grant any increase in salaries or other amounts payable, or to become payable by it, to any shareholder, officer, employee, agent, representative, or

    (b) Increase benefits payable to any officer, employee, agent, or representative, or

    (c) Modify any agreement, contract or commitment relating to the payment of wages, salaries, bonuses or other employee benefits; except that such increases may be granted to employees who are not officers in the ordinary course of business and consistent with past practices of the Corporation.

5.6 <u>Insurance</u>. The Corporation will continue in force its existing insurance coverage, subject only to variation in amounts required by the ordinary operations of its business.

5.7 <u>Change Contracts</u>. The Corporation will not modify, amend, cancel, or terminate any of its existing contracts or agreements, or agree to do any of those acts, except in the ordinary course of business.

5.8 <u>New Transactions</u>. The Corporation will not, without Buyer's prior written consent, do or agree to do any of the following acts:

(a) Enter into any contract, commitment, or transaction not in the usual and ordinary course of business; or

(b) Enter into any contract, commitment, or transaction in the usual and ordinary course of business involving any amount exceeding _____ Dollars ($____), or which requires the performance of services for more than a 12-month period; or

(c) Make any capital expenditures in excess of _____ Dollars ($____), or enter into any leases of capital equipment or property under which the annual lease charge is in excess of _____ Dollars ($_____);

(d) Sell or dispose of any capital assets;

(e) Mortgage, pledge or subject any of its business or assets to any lien, charge or encumbrance of any kind; or

(f) Extend credit to any third party other than in the ordinary course of business in accordance with its normal credit terms.

5.9 <u>Dividends, Distributions and Acquisitions of Stock</u>. The Corporation will not (a) declare, set aside or pay any dividend or make any distribution in respect of its capital stock; or (b) directly or indirectly purchase, redeem or otherwise acquire any shares of its capital stock; or (c) enter into any agreement obligating it to do any of the foregoing prohibited acts.

5.10   <u>Payment of Liabilities and Waiver of Claims</u>. The Corporation will not do, or agree to do, any of the following acts without the prior written approval of Buyer:

> (a) Pay any obligation or liability, fixed or contingent, other than current liabilities; or

> (b) Waive or compromise any right or claim; or

> (c) Cancel, without full payment, any note, loan or other obligation owing to the Corporation.

5.11   <u>Consents of Others</u>.   As soon as reasonably practical after the execution of this Agreement, and in any event on or before the Closing Date, the Shareholders and/or the Corporation will obtain the written consents of all agencies, persons or entities necessary to the consummation of the transactions contemplated by this Agreement.   In this regard, the Shareholders agree to immediately commence efforts to make all applications for regulatory approvals and to obtain all necessary third-party consents.

5.12   <u>Documentation of Procedures and Trade Secrets</u>. At Buyer's request, the Corporation will document and describe any of its trade secrets, processes or business procedures specified by Buyer, in form and content satisfactory to Buyer.

5.13 <u>Loans to or From Shareholders, Etc</u>. The Corporation will not borrow from or loan to its Shareholders, officers, directors or their spouses, children or relatives, any sums, and all amounts presently owed to such parties shall be fully repaid on or before the Closing Date.

5.14 <u>Other Borrowings</u>. Without Buyer's prior written consent, the Corporation shall not incur any additional debt other than trade debt incurred in the ordinary course of business and not exceeding $_____ in the aggregate.

5.15 <u>Continued Accuracy of Representations and Warranties</u>. The Shareholders will maintain the truth and accuracy of the representations and warranties contained in Section 3 of this Agreement and in any written statements delivered to Buyer by them. The Shareholders agree that they will notify Buyer in writing immediately upon any representation or warranty becoming inaccurate or untrue.

6.   <u>Buyer's Obligations Before Closing</u>.

6.1 <u>Consents and Approvals</u>. Buyer will cooperate with Shareholders in obtaining any necessary consents or approvals; provided, however, that Buyer shall not be obligated under this Section to execute any guaranty, assumption of liability, or other document or instrument requiring it to assume obligations not contemplated by this Agreement.

7.   <u>Conditions Precedent to Buyer's Obligations</u>.

All obligations of Buyer under this Agreement are subject to the satisfaction, on or before the Closing Date, of all of the conditions set forth below in this Section 7. Buyer may waive any or all of these conditions in whole or in part without prior notice; provided, however, that no such waiver of a condition shall constitute a waiver by Buyer of any of its other rights or remedies, at law or in equity, if Shareholders shall be in default of any of their representations, warranties, or covenants under this Agreement.

7.1 <u>Accuracy of Shareholders' Representations and Warranties</u>. The representations and warranties of the Shareholders in this Agreement, and in all certificates, documents and other written statements delivered by the Shareholders or the Corporation to Buyer pursuant hereto or in connection with the transactions contemplated hereby shall be true as of the Closing Date as though made at that time, except for changes permitted by this Agreement.

7.2 <u>Performance</u>.   The Shareholders and the Corporation shall have performed and complied in all material respects with all agreements, obligations and conditions required by this Agreement to be performed or complied with by them on or before the Closing Date.

7.3 <u>Consents</u>. All agreements, consents, approvals and licenses necessary for the consummation of the transactions contemplated by this Agreement, or otherwise pertaining to the matters covered by it, shall have been obtained by the Shareholders or the Corporation from the appropriate parties, including governmental agencies. Such consents shall include all required consents from the California Commissioner of Corporations.

7.4 <u>Absence of Litigation</u>. No suit, action, investigation, inquiry or other proceeding by a governmental body or other person or legal or administrative proceeding shall have been instituted or threatened which questions the validity or legality of the transactions contemplated hereby.

7.5 <u>Opinion of Counsel to Shareholders and Corporation</u>. The Shareholders shall have delivered to Buyer an opinion to the Shareholders and the Corporation, dated the Closing Date, in form and substance satisfactory to Buyer and its counsel.

7.6 <u>Approval of Documentation</u>. The form and substance of all certificates, instruments, opinions, and other documents delivered to Buyer under this Agreement shall be satisfactory in all reasonable respects to Buyer and its counsel.

7.7 <u>Resignations</u>. Shareholders shall have delivered to Buyer, except as otherwise requested by Buyer, the written resignations of all the officers and directors of the Corporation and will cause any other action to be taken with respect to these resignations that Buyer may reasonably request.

7.8 <u>Corporate Approval</u>. The execution and delivery of this Agreement by the Corporation and the performance of its covenants and obligations under it, shall have been duly authorized by all necessary corporate action, and Buyer shall have received copies of all resolutions pertaining to that authorization, certified by the secretary of the Corporation.

7.9 <u>Certification by Shareholders and Corporation</u>. Buyer shall have received a certificate, dated the Closing Date, signed and verified by the Shareholders and the Corporation's president and chief financial officer, certifying, in such detail as Buyer and its counsel may reasonably request, that [optional: to the best of their knowledge] the conditions specified in this Section have been fulfilled.

8.   <u>Conditions Precedent to the Shareholders' Obligations</u>.

The obligations of the Shareholders to sell and transfer the shares under this agreement are subject to the satisfaction on or before the Closing Date of all of the conditions set forth below in this Section 8. The Shareholders may waive any or all of there conditions in whole or in part without prior notice; provided, however, that no such waiver of a condition shall constitute a waiver by the Shareholders of any of their other rights or remedies, at law or in equity, if Buyer shall be in default of any of its representations, warranties or covenants under this Agreement.

8.1 <u>Representations and Warranties</u>. The representations and warranties of Buyer contained herein shall be true and accurate as of the Closing Date as though made at that time.

8.2 <u>Performance</u>. Buyer shall have performed and complied with all agreements, obligations and conditions required by this Agreement to be performed or complied with by it on or prior to the Closing Date.

8.3 <u>Opinion of Buyer's Counsel</u>. Buyer shall have furnished the Shareholders with an opinion of counsel for Buyer, in form and substance satisfactory to Shareholders.

8.4 <u>Corporate Approval</u>. The execution and delivery of this Agreement by Buyer and the performance of its covenants and obligations under it, shall have been duly authorized by all necessary corporate action, and the Shareholders shall have received copies of all resolutions pertaining to that authorization, certified by the secretary of the Buyer.

9.   <u>Closing</u>.

9.1 <u>Time and Place</u>. The consummation of the purchase and sale of the Shares, and all collateral transactions (the "Closing") shall occur at the offices of _____ at ___ local time, on _____, or at such other time and place as the parties may agree in writing (the "Closing Date").

9.2 <u>Deliveries and Following the Closing</u>. At the Closing, the respective parties hereto shall deliver all shares certificates, consents, estoppel certificates, checks and other instruments, opinions and documents provided for in this Agreement. In addition, the Shareholders covenant and agree (i) to deliver all books, records and documents and to take all actions as may be necessary or appropriate in order to deliver to Buyer full and complete title to and possession of the Corporation and its business and assets, and (ii) after the Closing Date, to execute and deliver all instruments and documents and perform all other acts which Buyer may reasonably request in order to further effect or perfect the sale and transfer of the shares and the consummation of the transactions contemplated in this Agreement.

10.   <u>Shareholders' Obligations After Closing</u>.

10.1   <u>Guaranty of Accounts Receivable</u>. The Shareholders jointly and severally guarantee to Buyer that the unpaid balance of all accounts receivable of the Corporation on had at the Closing Date will be paid during a collection period of ninety (90) days immediately following the Closing Date. Within ten (10) business days after delivery to the Shareholders of a schedule of all of these accounts receivable unpaid at the end of this collection period, the Shareholders will pay to Buyer the full amount of these unpaid receivables, in cash, less the amount reserved for doubtful accounts of $_____. Buyer will concurrently assign to the Shareholders the scheduled accounts, and all collections thereof by Buyer thereafter shall be remitted to the Shareholders. If more than one invoice is outstanding for any customer, the "first-in, first-out" principle shall be applied in determining the invoice to which a payment relates, unless the payment by its terms specifies or clearly indicates the invoice to which it relates.

10.2   <u>Shareholders' Indemnification</u>. The Shareholders hereby agree to jointly and severally indemnify, defend and hold harmless Buyer against and in respect of any and all claims, demands, losses, liabilities, costs, expenses, obligations and damages, including, without limitation, interest, penalties and reasonable attorneys' fees, suffered or incurred by Buyer which arise, result from or relate to any breach of or failure by the Shareholders to perform any of their representations, warranties, covenants or agreements in this Agreement, or in any schedule, certificate, exhibit or other instrument furnished or to be furnished under this Agreement.

Upon demand by Buyer for indemnification, the Shareholders shall forthwith pay to Buyer, in cash, the amount of the indemnification to which Buyer is entitled pursuant hereof. If such amount is not so paid, Buyer may offset such amount against the Note.

11.   <u>Buyer's Obligations After Closing</u>.

11.1   <u>Buyer's Indemnification</u>. Buyer hereby agrees to indemnify, defend and hold harmless the Shareholders against and in respect of any and all claims, demands, losses, liabilities, costs, expenses, obligations and damages, including, without limitation, interest, penalties and reasonable attorneys' fees, suffered or incurred by the Shareholders, which arise, result from or relate to any breach of or failure by Buyer to perform any of its representations, warranties, covenants or agreements in this Agreement or in any schedule, certificate, exhibit or other instrument furnished or to be furnished under this Agreement.

12. <u>Survival of Representations and Warranties</u>.

All representations, warranties, covenants, and agreements of the parties contained in this Agreement, or in any instrument, certificate opinion, schedule, exhibit or other writing provided for herein, shall survive the closing.

13. <u>Miscellaneous</u>.

13.1 <u>Expenses</u>. Each of the parties shall pay all costs and expenses incurred or to be incurred by it in negotiating and preparing this Agreement and in closing and carrying out the transactions contemplated by this Agreement.

13.2 <u>Notices and Deliveries</u>. All notices, requests, demands or other communications hereunder shall be in writing and shall be deemed to have been duly given on the date of service if served personally on the party to whom notice is to be given, or on the second day after mailing if mailed to the party to whom notices is to given by first class certified mail, return receipt requested, postage prepaid and addressed as follows:

(a) If to the Shareholders:

(b) It to Buyer:

Any party may, at any time, change its address for purposes of this Section by giving the other parties written notice of the new address in the manner set forth above.

13.3 <u>Attorneys' Fees</u>. In the event of any controversy or claim or dispute between the parties hereto arising out of or relating to this Agreement or any of the documents provided for herein, or the breach thereof, the prevailing party shall be entitled to recover from the losing party, reasonable attorneys' fees, expenses and costs.

13.4 <u>Binding Effect</u>. This Agreement shall be binding upon the successors and assigns of the respective parties hereto.

13.5 <u>Parties in Interest</u>. Nothing in this Agreement, whether express or implied, is intended to confer any rights or remedies under or by reason of this Agreement on any persons other than the parties to it and their respective successors and assigns, nor is anything in this Agreement intended to relieve or discharge the obligation or liability of any third persons to any party to this Agreement, nor shall any provision give any third persons any right of subrogation or action over against any party to this Agreement.

IN WITNESS WHEREOF, THIS AGREEMENT is executed and effective as of the date first written above.

"Buyer"

By :_____
_____, President

By :_____
_____, Secretary

"Shareholders"

_____

_____

ABOUT THE AUTHOR

KATHERINE L. DELSACK, J.D., LL.M.

Katherine L. Delsack, Esq. is a business attorney practicing in the Newport Beach, California area. She is a member of the bars of California and the District of Columbia and has been practicing tax and business law since 1982.

Immediately after graduating from law school she obtained a master's degree (LL.M) in taxation from Georgetown University in Washington, D.C. She is currently a member of the Executive Committee of the Business Law Section of the California State Bar and regularly serves as an arbitrator for the National Association of Securities Dealers.

She has served as Chairman of the International Law Committee for the General Practice Section of the American Bar Association and related tax sections of state bar associations. Ms. Delsack was also the Science and Technology Editor for the California Business Law Reporter.

Ms. Delsack is an adjunct faculty member at the University of California, Irvine (UCI) and Pepperdine University where she teaches in the M.B.A., Executive M.B.A., and Paralegal programs.

She is the author of numerous law journal articles as well as articles for non-legal, business periodicals. She has also authored and co-authored books for other legal publishers on related business law subjects.

Ms. Delsack has agreed to prepare initial incorporation documents, including the preparation of the securities forms for the issuance of stock for a total fee of $100.00 plus filing fees. For further information, she can be reached at LawPrep Press, Irvine, CA at (714) 261-8742.